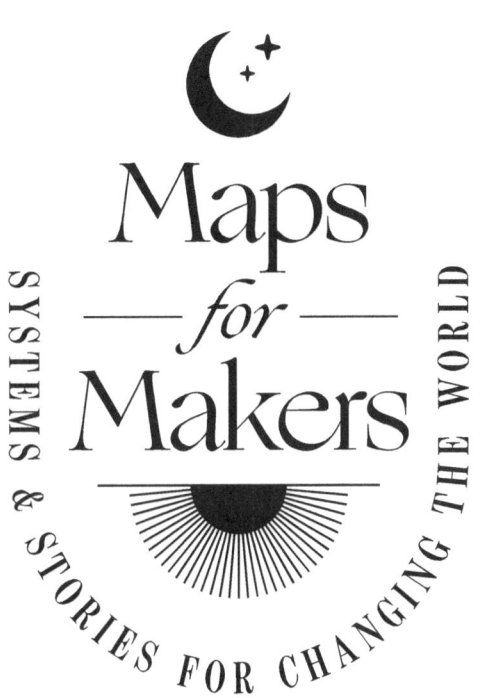

Maps for Makers

Rachel Collier
& Paul Lem, M.D.

MAPS FOR MAKERS:
SYSTEMS & STORIES FOR CHANGING THE WORLD

Copyright © by Rachel Collier & Paul Lem, M.D.
Design and Layout by Chris Di Lauro
Published by Third Door Stories
FIRST EDITION
ISBN: 9798671114508

All rights reserved. No part of this work may be reproduced or transmitted in any form or by any means, electronic or mechanical, including photocopying, recording, or by any information storage or retrieval system, without the prior written permission of the copyright owner and the publisher.

Trademarked names may appear in this book. Rather than use a trademark symbol with every occurrence of a trademarked name, we use the names only in an editorial fashion and to the benefit of the trademark owner, with no intention of infringement of the trademark.

The information in this book is distributed on an "as is" basis, without warranty. Although every precaution has been taken in the preparation of this work, neither the author nor publisher shall have any liability to any person or entity with respect to any loss or damage caused or alleged to be caused directly or indirectly by the information contained in this work.

For Elizabeth

Contents

INTRODUCTION	3
LEARNING TO LEARN	5
DAILY HABITS	17
TIME MANAGEMENT	39
CREATIVE PROBLEM SOLVING	47
FINANCIAL FREEDOM	53
LOVE YOUR WORK	67
WORK WORTH DOING	75
WINNING STRATEGY	83
ASSEMBLE A GREAT TEAM	93
CONCLUSION	107
REFERENCES	111

Introduction

BY RACHEL COLLIER

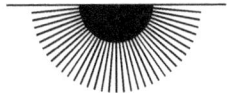

This is a book about magic. I know because I am an expert on magic.

When I was growing up, I read every book I could get my hands on. My favorite was Harry Potter. I loved how he escaped from mean muggles. I loved how Hogwarts trained him to use magic. And I loved how a handful of resourceful witches and wizards defeated Lord Voldemort.

In university, I studied journalism because I wanted to share stories like the ones in Harry Potter. Stories about the underdog coming out on top. Stories about regular people discovering their power to help themselves and others.

After I graduated, I needed to pay off my student loans. Reluctantly, I joined a biotech start-up founded by Dr. Paul Lem. Paul told me he was starting a school called Raven Dojo for young entrepreneurs to change the world.

He asked, "Would you like to join?"

I was skeptical.

I challenged him, "What makes you think you can change the world?"

He replied, "Great question. You tell me. How can we change the world?"

I didn't know the answer. But I wanted to learn. Badly. I wanted to fix the big broken things. Education. Healthcare. Racism. Sexism. In short, I wanted to learn true magic.

Paul and I spent the next several years analyzing thousands of scientific articles and case studies about changing the world.

Gradually, we collected a system of mental maps—maps for making a difference.

We wrote this book to share them with you. What do you have to lose? An hour of your time. What do you have to gain? The rest of your life.

> *"Help will always be given at Hogwarts to those who ask for it."*
>
> **-J.K. Rowling**

MAP 1

Learning to Learn

The man raises his bow and draws the arrow, holding it against the bowstring in effortless tension. He feels the same easy tension in his breath as he sets his eyes upon the straw target. He empties his mind and waits. Suddenly, the arrow is loosed from the bow and his teacher shouts, "It is there!" The archer has finally hit his mark.

In 1924, philosophy professor Eugen Herrigel was determined to learn the Japanese art of archery. His friends were skeptical—Europeans rarely succeeded. But with the help of a colleague at the University of Tokyo, Herrigel convinced master Kenzo Awa to take him as a pupil.

Their training began. Awa showed him how the arrow must fly smoothly and effortlessly from the bow like "snow from a bamboo leaf." But Herrigel could hardly even draw the 6-foot bow without his muscles failing. For hours each day, his master patiently pointed out mistakes and adjusted his technique. After a year, Herrigel learned how to draw the bow. After several years, he could shoot jerky wobbly arrows into the air.

Four years into his training, Herrigal was frustrated by his lack of progress. He accused Awa of being a charlatan. In response, his teacher placed a stick the width of a knitting needle into the sand and turned off the lights. When Herrigel retrieved the stick, there were two arrows in it—the second embedded in the first. Herrigel was now a believer and devoted himself to practice.

Finally, in his fifth year of training, Herrigel mastered the art of archery. His arrows truly flew like snow from bamboo leaves. After he passed his final test, his master said, "Now at last, the bowstring has cut right through you."

The road to mastery is difficult. It requires tremendous practice, failure, and perseverance. But the reward is world-class skills to change the world. This Map is designed to help you learn the essential skills as quickly as possible so you can make a difference.

> *Never let formal education get in the way of your learning.*
> —**Mark Twain**

> *Development is a series of rebirths.*
> —**Maria Montessori**

GOAL

Achieve expert-level performance in the shortest amount of time with the least amount of effort.

WHY?

It's faster and easier to change the world when you have world-class skills.

HOW?

Phase 1

- Achieve 80% mastery with a proven system
- Time: 1-2 hours/day for a few months to a few years

Phase 2

- Master the remaining 20% with competition and coaching
- Time: 4 hours/day of deliberate practice for 10 years

It isn't the learning that's so hard, but the unlearning.

-**Charlie Munger**

The illiterate of the twenty-first century will not be those who cannot read and write, but those who cannot learn, unlearn, and relearn.

-**Alvin Toffler**

PHASE 1:
Intermediate

Step 1: Find the proven system
- In most fields, there is a proven system that allows beginners to quickly reach intermediate-level performance
- Find it by asking experts and noting which one keeps getting recommended
- The proven system doesn't have to be expensive—it is often free or available in a book
- Examples of proven systems:
    - Paleolithic diet for nutrition and weight loss
    - Total Immersion (TI) for long-distance swimming
    - Consultative selling systems such as *SPIN Selling* by Neil Rackham
    - Toastmasters for public speaking
    - *How to Win Friends and Influence People* by Dale Carnegie for social skills
    - *On Writing Well* by William Zinsser for clear writing
    - *The Artist's Way* by Julia Cameron for creativity
    - Meditation for attention and clarity
    - *Maps for Makers* for changing the world

Step 2: Practice the system

- Practice the system until you can perform the actions automatically without thinking
    - e.g., when you're learning to drive a car, you have to think consciously about each action. With practice, you can drive a car automatically.
    - Performance suffers when you think consciously because it slows your reaction time
        - e.g., most people have a reaction time of 0.25 seconds. When asked to consciously perform a task, reaction time slows to 0.75 seconds.
        - e.g., tennis player John McEnroe would compliment opponents on their best stroke as they changed sides on the court. This caused them to think consciously and play worse.
        - e.g., people perceive you as less honest when you pause to think before responding
    - The goal is to achieve a peak state of performance called "flow"
        - Flow is when you are totally immersed in an activity that stretches your skills to the limit. This state is highly enjoyable and feels like "time is flying" because it engages both your conscious mind and subconscious mind. People in flow often create work they did not think possible.
        - Flow requires your skill level to match the difficulty level. You'll be bored if your skill is high and the activity is easy. Likewise, you'll be frustrated if your skill is low and the task is hard.
            - e.g., you are bored by biking along a paved path, but you are in flow when you bike down a mountain and have to focus moment to moment on avoiding trees and rocks
            - This means you need to increase the difficulty level as your skill increases

- Example:
  - In ancient Japan, Musashi Miyamoto and other legendary samurai achieved a state of mind known as *mushin no shin*, a Zen expression meaning *mind of no mind*
    - It refers to an absence of anger, fear, or ego. There is no thinking or judging. You are free to act and react without hesitation.
  - Swordsmen trained for years to achieve mushin, repeating the same movements until they could perform them spontaneously without conscious thought
  - With his mastery of mushin, Miyamoto was undefeated in more than 60 duels

Flow is being completely involved in an activity for its own sake. The ego falls away. Time flies. Every action, movement, and thought follows inevitably from the previous one, like playing jazz.

-Mihaly Csikszentmihalyi

It is rarely a mysterious technique that drives us to the top, but rather a profound mastery of what may well be a basic skill set.

-Josh Waitzkin

PHASE 2:
Expert

Step 1: Get real-world feedback
- Examples:
  - Enter a competition and see how you rank
  - Launch a product and see if anyone buys it
  - Create a company and see if anyone invests in it

- - Set measurable goals and track whether you achieve them
- Everyone is biased. Reality reveals your true strengths and weaknesses.
  - Your left brain constantly generates stories to explain why you act and feel the way you do, but these stories are often inaccurate
    - e.g., google "list of cognitive biases" to see the common traps people fall into
- After you master one level of competition, move to the next level
  - When you start a new level, it can be frustrating to lose, especially when you're used to winning
    - Develop a "growth mindset" where you view failure as an opportunity to learn and try again
      - Researchers have found that even geniuses like Shakespeare and Thomas Edison had many more failures than successes and their odds of success depended on how many times they tried
- Example:
  - In the movie *Edge of Tomorrow*, Major William Cage dies and is reborn over and over again until he masters the skills to fight alien invaders
    - Real-world competition for survival (along with Sergeant Rita Vrataski's gentle training) transforms him from a coward to a warrior

The entire exercise of Vipassana meditation is to learn the difference between fiction and reality, what is real and what is just stories that we invent and construct in our own minds. Almost 99 percent you realize is just stories in our minds.

-**Yuval Noah Harari**

It is not the critic who counts; not the man who points out how the strong man stumbles, or where the doer of deeds could have done them better. The credit belongs to the man who is actually in the arena, whose face is marred by dust and sweat and blood; who strives valiantly; who errs, who comes short again and again, because there is no effort without error and shortcoming; but who does actually strive to do the deeds; who knows great enthusiasms, the great devotions; who spends himself in a worthy cause; who at the best knows in the end the triumph of high achievement, and who at the worst, if he fails, at least fails while daring greatly, so that his place shall never be with those cold and timid souls who neither know victory nor defeat.

-Theodore Roosevelt

Step 2: Practice for 4 hours/day

- Use real-world feedback to create specific exercises that fix your weaknesses and develop your strengths
  - This process is called "deliberate practice" and it greatly accelerates improvement
  - e.g., martial arts champion Josh Waitzkin filmed his matches and painstakingly analyzed each frame to discover his errors
- Rest and recover
  - e.g., get 7-8 hours of restful sleep every night
- The end result is you'll have one or two world-class strengths and no obvious weaknesses
  - e.g., at the age of 35, near the end of his tennis career, Roger Federer debuted an improved backhand and won 19 of his next 20 matches, including defeating his nemesis Rafael Na-

dal three times in a row. In previous matches, Nadal won by relentlessly attacking Federer's weak one-handed backhand.
  - At high levels of competition, you often only have to be slightly better than everyone else to reap most of the rewards
    - This is because there is usually only a small difference in talent between experts
    - e.g., this "tournament effect" explains why Beyoncé earned $105 million in 2017, compared to only $56,000 for the average musician

With deliberate practice, however, the goal is not just to reach your potential but to build it, to make things possible that were not possible before. This requires challenging homeostasis—getting out of your comfort zone—and forcing your brain or your body to adapt.

-**Anders Ericsson**

We've come to believe that world-class performance comes after 10,000 hours of practice. But that's wrong. It comes after 10,000 hours of deliberate practice, 12,500 hours of deliberate rest, and 30,000 hours of sleep.

-**Alex Soojung-Kim Pang**

Step 3: Get a coach
- Find potential coaches by asking top performers for their recommendations
  - The ideal coach is someone who deeply understands the field and also deeply understands you
    - e.g., "Zen master" Phil Jackson has won 11 NBA championships as a coach, including 6 with the Chicago Bulls. In his autobiography *Eleven Rings: The Soul of Success*, he

reveals his deep understanding by explaining things such as the "triangle offence" and the psychology of superstars like Michael Jordan, Scottie Pippen, and Dennis Rodman.
  - Note that if you can't find a living coach, you can look to history to find your perfect teacher
    - e.g., Charlie Munger says: "I am a biography nut myself. And I think when you're trying to teach the great concepts that work, it helps to tie them into the lives and personalities of the people who developed them. I think you learn economics better if you make Adam Smith your friend. That sounds funny, making friends among the eminent dead, but if you go through life making friends with the eminent dead who had the right ideas, I think it will work better in life and work better in education. It's way better than just being given the basic concepts."
- Test potential coaches by describing a problem you're trying to solve and asking for ideas. Choose the coach whose ideas work best for you.
  - Your track record of success in competitions will help convince a top coach to train you
    - The best coaches are always looking for students who have the potential to be world champions
- Your coach will design a personalized practice program that helps you win
  - e.g., at age 17, Mikaela Shiffrin became the youngest American skier to win a World Cup. Her mom Eileen trained her with exercises such as juggling while riding a unicycle to develop her balance and coordination.

When the student is ready, the teacher will appear.
-Buddhist proverb

I cannot teach anybody anything. I can only make them think.

-Socrates

Every blade of grass has its Angel that bends over it and whispers, "Grow, grow."

-The Talmud

We were kids without fathers...so we found our fathers on wax and on the streets and in history. We got to pick and choose the ancestors who would inspire the world we were going to make for ourselves.

-Jay-Z

Example: Henry Ford
- In 1879, Henry Ford left his family farm at age 16 to apprentice in the machine shops of Detroit, where he learned the fundamentals of engines and how to run a business
- In 1891, he got a job at Edison Illuminating Company and was promoted to chief engineer within 3 years because of his hard work and innovative strategies
- In 1896, Ford showed his plans for a "horseless carriage" to Thomas Edison, who was so impressed that he became Ford's lifelong mentor
- In 1908, Ford changed the world by launching the "Model T"—the first affordable consumer automobile

Failure is the opportunity to begin again, more intelligently.

-Henry Ford

NOTE: It's easier to learn if you believe in yourself
- Self-efficacy is the psychological term for believing in your ability to get something done
- This "I can do it" mindset makes you resilient to setbacks
- Here are three ways to strengthen your "I can do it" mindset:
    - Develop a growth mindset
        - A growth mindset is the belief that you can change your qualities through hard work and learning
        - Strengthen your "I can improve" mindset by noticing and re-framing your "I can't improve" thoughts
            - e.g., "Some people are born to do great things and I'm not one of them" becomes "I don't feel like I can change the world right now but I know I can train to become ready"
            - Mindfulness meditation teaches you how to observe your thoughts
    - Achieve mastery experiences
        - A mastery experience is when you successfully achieve something
            - It's the most effective way of strengthening your "I can do it" mindset because it's real-life evidence that you have what it takes to succeed
        - Achieve mastery experiences by setting actionable goals that are moderately challenging and seeking concrete feedback to improve your skills
            - e.g., for most people, becoming financially free in 5 years is a better challenge than trying to do it in 5 months
    - Find role models
        - Seeing other people like you achieve success strengthens your belief that you can do it too
        - That's why you should surround yourself with other social

- leaders and entrepreneurs who want to change the world
  - If it's hard to find people like this in your life, you can learn from the lives of role models throughout history

The mind is everything; what you think, you become.

-Buddha

There is nothing either good or bad, but thinking makes it so.

-William Shakespeare

Suggested reading

- *Zen in the Art of Archery* by Eugen Herrigel
- *Mindset: The New Psychology of Success* by Carol Dweck
- *The Art of Learning: An Inner Journey to Optimal Performance* by Josh Waitzkin

Next steps

Now that you understand the system for learning new things, it's time to implement it. The next Map will show you how the power of habit can dramatically improve your life..

MAP 2

Daily Habits

*I*n 2002, Britain's top cyclists were notoriously bad. They had never won a Tour de France. They kept losing at the Olympics (only one gold medal in 76 years). And the best manufacturers refused to sell bicycles to the national team because they were such big losers.

In 2003, everything changed. The British Cycling Federation hired a coach named Dave Brailsford. Dave had no coaching experience. But he did have new ideas based on his experiences as a former cyclist and bicycle distributor. The results were spectacular. At the 2008 Beijing Olympics, Britain won 8 gold medals. In 2012, a British cyclist won the Tour de France for the first time. It wasn't a fluke—Britain went on to win the next three Tours.

What did Dave do differently? He optimized every factor that could impact performance. Dave's cyclists practiced in wind tunnels to find the most aerodynamic clothing. He painted floors white to spot dust interfering with bicycle maintenance. A surgeon trained his cyclists to wash their hands properly to not get sick. His team traveled with their own mattresses so they could sleep in the same position every night.

Dave called his strategy "the aggregation of marginal gains." While each new optimization might improve performance by only 1%, the sum of all optimizations compounded for a huge improvement. While other people ignored these small areas for improvement, Dave and his team mastered them—and it led to years of spectacular wins.

This example shows the power of habits. By making a series of small changes, you can massively improve your performance.

> *A daily routine built on good habits and disciplines separates the most successful among us from everyone else.*
> **-Darren Hardy**

> *Be regular and orderly in your life, so that you may be violent and original in your work.*
> **-Gustave Flaubert**

> *The effects of compounding even moderate returns over many years are compelling, if not downright mind boggling.*
> **-Seth Klarman**

GOAL
Prepare your mind and body to take on the world's biggest challenges.

HOW?
Implement the following system of 9 daily habits:

1. Exercise for 30 minutes
2. Meditate for 15 minutes
3. Write 3 pages of stream of consciousness
4. Eat a Paleo diet of protein, fat, fruits, and vegetables
5. Schedule 1 hour of uninterrupted time for your most important project
6. Take two 10-minute walk breaks
7. Read for 30 minutes
8. Do a gratitude exercise
9. Get a good night's sleep

WHY?

These habits are scientifically proven to make you happier, healthier, and smarter.

These habits reinforce each other so that the system is more than the sum of its parts.

- e.g., exercise improves sleep, which improves attention, which helps you work on your important project

Once they are adopted by your subconscious mind, habits are performed automatically, which means your self-control and willpower can be used for other choices and decisions.

> *We are what we repeatedly do. Excellence, then, is not an act, but a habit.*
> **-Aristotle**

> *Losers have goals. Winners have systems.*
> **-Scott Adams**

HOW DO I TURN ACTIONS INTO HABITS?

Habits have three parts:

1. Cue: a trigger that initiates the action
    - e.g., location, time, emotional state, other people
2. Routine: the action that you do
3. Reward: the benefit from doing the action

Design your cues and optimize the rewards to reinforce a new routine

- e.g., put your running shoes by your bed as a cue to run when you wake up
- e.g., record your run in a calendar and feel a sense of accomplishment when you see that you ran every day for 2 weeks in a row

Note that it takes about 6-10 weeks to turn a daily action into a habit.

Note that it is difficult to adopt an entirely new set of habits, so start small and build on your system.

- e.g., start with the meditation and writing habits and then add a new one each month

Motivation is what gets you started. Habit is what keeps you going.

-Jim Rohn

Example daily schedule

6:30 am	Wake up and expose your eyes to bright light
6:30-7:00am	Exercise
7:00-7:15am	Meditate
7:15-7:45 am	Write 3 pages of stream of consciousness
7:45-8:00am	Eat a Paleo breakfast with protein and fruit
8:00-9:00 am	Work for 1 hour on your most important project
11:00-11:10am	Take a walk break
12:00-12:15pm	Eat a Paleo lunch with protein and vegetables
3:00-3:10pm	Take a walk break
6:00-6:15pm	Eat a Paleo dinner with protein and vegetables
10:00-10:30pm	Read
10:30-10:35pm	Do a gratitude exercise
11:00pm	Go to bed
Total time	3 hours, 55 minutes (24% of your waking hours)

HABIT 1:
Exercise for 30 minutes

WHY?

Exercise improves your mind and body so you can help others better.

Scientifically-proven benefits of regular exercise:
- Healthier
    - Longer life
    - Lower risk of heart attack, stroke, and heart failure
    - Lower risk of Alzheimer's disease
    - Less anxiety and depression
    - Lower risk of diabetes
    - Lower risk of cancer
    - Better sleep
    - Better endurance, strength, flexibility, and balance
- Smarter
    - Better memory
    - Better attention
    - Faster cognitive processing speed
    - Greater self-control
- Happier
    - Better mood
    - Less depression

Those who think they have not time for bodily exercise will sooner or later have to find time for illness.

                                                            -Edward Stanley, Earl of Derby

HOW?

Do 30 minutes of exercise every day
- 20 minutes of resistance training every day
- 10 minutes of aerobic exercise one day, alternating with 10 minutes of balance/coordination/flexibility training the other day

Resistance training
- Exercise your major muscle groups twice per week: chest, arms, back, shoulders, legs
- Rest for at least 2 days before exercising the same muscle group
- Lifting to failure builds the most muscle
    - e.g., lots of repetitions of low weight or a few repetitions of high weight
- Eat protein immediately after exercising to build muscle
- If you don't have access to a gym, you can do high-intensity circuit training using your body weight
    - e.g., there are hundreds of high-intensity interval training (HIIT) YouTube workouts you can do in your living room

Aerobic training
- To get a good workout in 10 minutes, do interval training where you alternate high-intensity exercise that elevates your heart rate with low-intensity exercise that lets you recover
    - e.g., repeat 30 seconds of sprinting followed by 2 minutes of walking

Balance/coordination/flexibility training
- Do 10 minutes of yoga or tai chi
- Hold each posture for 30 seconds to get the best stretch

Habit forming
- Record your exercise every day in a calendar that is posted where you can easily see it
- Create highly-visible cues to trigger you to exercise
    - e.g., put a motivational exercise quote in your kitchen

> *The doctor of the future will give no medication, but will interest his patients in the care of the human frame, diet and in the cause and prevention of disease.*
>
> *-Thomas A. Edison*

Warning

It's a good idea to talk to your doctor before starting a new exercise routine. If you're not in good shape, start slowly and increase your intensity over time.

HABIT 2:
Meditate for 15 minutes

WHY?

Meditation improves your mind

- It helps you improve your attention so you can be more efficient
- It helps you observe your thoughts so you can choose better things to be efficient about

Other scientifically-proven benefits of mindfulness meditation:

- Better memory
- Stronger immune system
- Less anxiety, depression, fatigue, and pain
- Less stress

> *The gift of learning to meditate is the greatest gift you can give yourself in this lifetime.*
>
> *-Sogyal Rinpoche*

> *When meditation is mastered, the mind is unwavering like the flame of a candle in a windless place.*
>
> *-Bhagavad Gita*

HOW?

Sogyal Rinpoche is a Tibetan lama and the founder of Rigpa, a network of Buddhist centers around the world. In *The Tibetan Book of Living and Dying*, he offers advice on how to start meditating:

Posture

1. Sit with your back straight, like an arrow or a pile of golden coins.
2. The lower part of your spine has a natural curve; it should be relaxed but upright.
3. Balance your head comfortably on your neck.
4. Your shoulders and the upper part of your torso should be held in a strong poise, but without any tension.
5. Sit with your legs crossed. You may also choose to sit on a chair with your legs relaxed. Be sure to keep your back straight.
6. Keep your eyes open so you don't fall asleep.
7. When your mind is restless, calm it down by lowering your gaze. When your mind is dull and sleepy, bring your gaze up to increase alertness.
8. Do not focus on anything in particular. Instead, turn back slightly into yourself. Let your gaze expand, and become more spacious and pervasive.
9. Keep your mouth slightly open, as if you were about to say a deep and relaxing "Aaaah". Breathe mainly through your mouth.

Meditation

10. Observe your breathing. Rest your attention, lightly and mindfully, on your breath.
11. Breathe naturally, just as you always do.
12. Focus your awareness lightly on your outbreath.
13. Each time you breathe out, you will find there is a natural gap before you breathe in again.
14. Rest in that gap, in the open space.

15. Do not concentrate too much on your breath. Give it about 25 percent of your attention. Focus the other 75 percent on being quiet and spaciously relaxed.
16. Do not try to control your mind. Let peace come naturally, without effort.
17. Balance yourself between relaxation and alertness.
18. A beginner should start with short sessions. Practice for 4–5 minutes, then take a 1-minute break before starting again.
19. Over time, the contrast between meditation and everyday life will gradually dissolve. More and more, you will find yourself in your natural pure presence, without distraction.

Habit forming
- Record your meditation every day in a calendar that is posted where you can easily see it
- Create a highly-visible cue to trigger you to meditate
  - e.g., put a motivational meditation quote in your kitchen

The purpose of meditation practice is not enlightenment; it is to pay attention even at extraordinary times, to be of the present, nothing-but-in-the-present, to bear this mindfulness of now into each event of ordinary life.

-Peter Matthiessen

HABIT 3:
Write 3 pages of stream of consciousness

WHY?
Stream of consciousness writing allows your subconscious thoughts to rise into your conscious mind.

This greatly increases your creativity and helps you observe your true nature.

Other scientifically-proven benefits of stream of consciousness writing:
- Higher happiness
- More meaning in life
- Fewer negative thoughts
- Better planning

HOW?

Set aside 15-30 minutes every morning where you can write uninterrupted.

Create a password-protected, double-spaced Word document.

Write whatever comes into your mind until you have filled 3 pages.

If you're feeling blocked about something in your life, try asking yourself questions and writing the first answer that comes to mind.

For more information, read about "Morning Pages" in Julia Cameron's book *The Artist's Way*.

Habit forming
- Create highly-memorable cues to trigger your writing
    - e.g., write while you drink your morning coffee
    - e.g., keep your Word document saved on your desktop

Pages clarify our yearnings. They keep an eye on our goals. They may provoke us, coax us, comfort us, even cajole us, as well as prioritize and synchronize the day at hand. If we are drifting, the pages will point that out. They will point the way True North. Each morning, as we face the page, we meet ourselves. The pages give us a place to vent and a place to dream. They are intended for no eyes but our own.

-Julia Cameron

HABIT 4:
Eat a Paleo diet of protein, fats, fruits, and vegetables

WHY?

For 2.6 million years, our Paleolithic ancestors ate a diet high in wild animal protein and fat

- Agriculture was invented only 11,000 years ago
  - Before then, there were no simple carbohydrates like wheat, rice, pasta, flour, potatoes, and refined sugar
- Dairy foods such as milk and cheese were invented only 6,000 years ago

Similar to Paleolithic people, modern-day hunter-gatherers eat a diet high in wild animal protein and fat with some gathered plant foods

- Their average Body Mass Index (BMI) is 19-22 and there are no overweight or obese people
  - Note that BMI does not distinguish between fat and muscle, so it is possible to be outside this range and still be healthy
- They have a low incidence of diseases such as diabetes and heart disease

Scientifically-proven benefits of eating a Paleo diet:

- Healthier
  - You will naturally achieve a healthy BMI of 19-22
  - Longer life
  - Lower risk of diabetes, heart disease, and cancer

- Lower blood pressure and cholesterol
- Smarter
    - Better memory, attention, and cognitive performance
- Happier
    - Higher happiness and life satisfaction
    - Less negative emotions, poor mood, and fatigue

Let food be your medicine and medicine be your food.

-Hippocrates

HOW?

For protein, eat chicken, fish, eggs, nuts, legumes, pasture-fed red meat, and wild meat

- Limit the amount of grain-fed beef
- Limit the amount of grain-fed pork
- Limit the amount of cheese and unsweetened yogurt
- Limit the amount of processed meat

For fat, eat omega-3 fats and unsaturated fats

- e.g., wild and farmed salmon is high in omega 3
- e.g., nuts and olive oil are high in unsaturated fat
- Avoid trans fats completely

For fruits, eat raw whole fruits

- Avoid fruit juice and other processed fruit

For vegetables, eat non-starchy vegetables

- Limit the amount of starchy vegetables
    - e.g., potatoes
- Avoid processed vegetable foods

For beverages, drink water or unsweetened tea or coffee
- Limit the amount of 2% or whole milk
- Don't drink skim or 1% milk
  - There's not enough fat to slow down the absorption of lactose sugar

Avoid foods containing simple carbohydrates
- e.g., bread, pasta, rice, chips, cookies, cake

Avoid foods containing sugar
- e.g., soft drinks, candy

Eat a mix of protein, fat, and vegetables with every meal
- Eat until you're full
- Add more protein if you're hungry in between meals

Habit forming
- Create highly-visible cues that trigger you to eat a Paleo diet
  - e.g., fill your fridge and freezer with only protein, fruits, and vegetables
  - e.g., put fruits and vegetables in a glass bowl in your kitchen

Breaking the rules
- Your health and weight won't be significantly affected if you break the rules less than 10% of the time
- If you do indulge, eat something you really enjoy
  - e.g., lemon cookies are one of the great joys in life

Don't eat anything your great grandmother wouldn't recognize as food.

-Michael Pollan

EXAMPLES

Breakfast

- Oatmeal + peanut butter + banana
- Scrambled eggs + avocado + tomatoes

Lunch and dinner

- Roast chicken + salad + tomatoes
- Baked salmon + stir-fried vegetables

Snacks

- Nuts
- Fruits
- Vegetable sticks

Dessert

- Fruits

> *The promotion of low-fat diets was a 40-year fad, with disastrous outcomes, conceived of, authorized, and policed by nutritionists.*
>
> **-Ian Leslie**

HABIT 5:
Schedule 1 hour of uninterrupted time for your most important project

WHY?

This guarantees you will make progress every day on your project.

WHY 1 HOUR?

It's hard to maintain your attention for more than 1 hour

- If you notice your attention dropping off, take a 1-minute break
    - e.g., set your computer's desktop background to a nature photo and visualize yourself relaxing in the scene
    - e.g., get a drink of water
    - e.g., get up and stretch
- Get a warm, bright light for your desk to improve your attention

I decided I would sell myself the best hour of the day to improving my own mind, and the world could buy the rest of the time. It sounds selfish, but it worked.
            -**Charlie Munger**

If you work on something a little bit every day, you end up with something that is massive.
            -**Kenneth Goldsmith**

WHY UNINTERRUPTED TIME?

It's important to focus on one thing and finish it because multi-tasking results in poorer performance than doing one task at a time

- It takes time and mental effort to switch your attention from an unfinished task to a new one

Background noise like music and other people's conversations disrupts your attention, memory, and learning.

Concentrate all your thoughts upon the work at hand. The sun's rays do not burn until brought to a focus.
            -**Alexander Graham Bell**

HOW?

Schedule the 1-hour time in your calendar
- Ideally, it will be at the same time every day so you get accustomed to it
- For more tips, check out the Map for "Time Management" (page 39)

Block out background noise
- e.g., close your office door
- e.g., use earphones and listen to the same song on repeat

Block out interruptions
- e.g., turn off notifications on your phone
- e.g., turn off email notifications for your online email browser

> *Work is hard. Distractions are plentiful. And time is short.*
> —**Adam Hochschild**

HABIT 6:
Take two 10-minute walk breaks

WHY?

Scientifically-proven benefits of taking restful breaks:
- Higher energy
- Better attention
- More creativity
- Less muscle strain
- More positive emotions

> *Thoughts come clearly while one walks.*
> —**Thomas Mann**

HOW?

Take a 10-minute walk break in the morning and another one in the afternoon

- You'll feel more refreshed if you take a walk in nature
- Expose yourself to more nature back at the office
    - e.g., set your desktop background to a nature scene

Habit forming

- Create a highly-visible cue that triggers you to take your walks
    - e.g., put a motivational walking quote on your desk
    - e.g., put an event in your calendar so you remember not to book back-to-back meetings

Your calm mind is the ultimate weapon against your challenges. So relax.

-Bryant McGill

HABIT 7:
Read for 30 minutes

WHY?

Scientifically-proven benefits of reading more:

- Larger vocabulary and better spelling
- More general knowledge
- Ability to read faster
- Better brainpower in old age

Reading is to the mind what exercise is to the body.

-Richard Steele

We read a lot. I don't know anyone who's wise who doesn't read a lot. But that's not enough: You have to have a temperament to grab ideas and do sensible things. Most people don't grab the right ideas or don't know what to do with them.

-Charlie Munger

HOW?

Schedule time to read for 30 minutes every day.

If you're not sure what to read, start with the book recommendations at the end of each chapter in this book.

Remember life is short—if you aren't enjoying a book, pick a new one.

Habit forming
- Create a highly-visible cue that triggers you to read
  - e.g., put a book on your pillow

When you read, you can absorb the entire life of another person in a few days.

-James Altucher

Learn every day, but especially from the experiences of others. It's cheaper!

-John C. Bogle

HABIT 8:
Do a gratitude exercise

WHY?

It is human nature to focus your attention on negative events rather than positive ones, but gratitude trains you to focus on the positive.

Scientifically-proven benefits of regularly doing a gratitude exercise:
- Higher happiness
- Better sleep
- Lower blood pressure
- Less stress

> *Gratitude is not only the greatest of virtues, but the parent of all others.*
> **-Marcus Tullius Cicero**

> *Most human beings have an almost infinite capacity for taking things for granted.*
> **-Aldous Huxley**

HOW?

Before you go to bed, review your day and think of something that makes you feel grateful
- e.g., it could be a person, thing, or event
- Doing this exercise before bed primes your subconscious to focus on positive thoughts while you sleep

Habit forming
- Create a highly-visible cue that triggers you to do the gratitude exercise
    - e.g., keep your gratitude journal by your bed or saved on your desktop

> *Gratitude can transform common days into thanksgivings, turn routine jobs into joy and change ordinary opportunities into blessings.*
>
> -William Arthur Ward

HABIT 9:
Get a good night's sleep

WHY?

Being well rested will give you the energy and brain power you need to change the world.

Scientifically-proven benefits of a good night's sleep:

- Healthier
    - Faster reaction time and better physical performance
    - Stronger immune system and less illness
    - Lower risk of diabetes
    - Less stress hormones
    - Higher testosterone for men
    - Lower risk of dying in traffic accidents
- Smarter
    - Better memory
    - Better attention and concentration
    - Greater self-control
    - Faster learning
    - More creative insights
- Better social skills
    - Greater emotional control
    - Better at reading facial expressions

- Happier
    - More positive emotions
    - More relaxed
    - Higher self-acceptance
    - Greater personal growth

You're not healthy, unless your sleep is healthy.

-**Dr. William Dement**

HOW?

Sleep 7-9 hours every night

- Set the temperature lower at night to help you sleep

Go to bed and wake up at the same time every day to maintain your 24-hour circadian rhythm.

When you wake up, expose your eyes to bright sunlight to reset your melatonin levels

- During fall, winter, and spring, it's dark in the morning so use a 10,000 lux bright light lamp
    - e.g., Verilux HappyLight®
    - For fastest results, close your eyes and hold them right up to the lamp for 60 seconds every morning

Habit forming

- Set a daily alarm for 15 minutes before bedtime to give yourself time to wind down and get ready for bed
- Create a highly-visible cue that triggers you to expose your eyes to bright light in the morning
    - e.g., put the Verilux HappyLight® beside your bed so you see it when you wake up

In the end, winning is sleeping better.

-Jodie Foster

Suggested reading
- *Master Life Faster: How to be Happy, Healthy, Wealthy, Smart & Social* by Paul Lem, M.D.
- *The Power of Habit: Why We Do What We Do in Life and Business* by Charles Duhigg
- *Atomic Habits* by James Clear

Next steps

Habits have the power to massively improve your life. But often, people don't stick to new habits because they don't feel like they have enough time in a day. What if you had enough time to do anything you ever wanted or needed to do? The next Map solves this problem.

MAP 3
Time Management

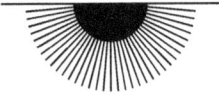

The poet opens his eyes and starts writing: "In Xanadu did Kubla Khan..." He feels like he's still dreaming. He wanders through an ancient forest and stands at the edge of a deep chasm. He hears voices warning of war with a terrible lord: "Beware! Beware! His flashing eyes, his floating hair!"

Far away, there is a sharp sound. He tries to ignore it, but the knocking grows louder. The vision fades. He's back in his study. Annoyed, he gets up and answers the door.

Samuel Taylor Coleridge never finished his poem. By the time the visitor left, his inspiration was gone. Even unfinished, *Kubla Khan* is one of the greatest works of English literature. But what if Coleridge had ignored the interruption? What if he had continued writing the poem as it flowed out of his mind?

Today, you face more distractions than ever. This Map will show you how to free your time so you can finish your masterpiece.

Time is the substance of life. When anyone asks you to give your time, they're really asking for a chunk of your life.

-Antoinette Bosco

WHY?

A time management system saves time and improves your creativity and conscientiousness

- Creativity is best when your mind is clear and not under time pressure
- Conscientiousness is being organized and on time

Scientifically-proven benefits of conscientiousness:

- Longer life
- Less stress
- Better sleep
- More positive emotions and higher life satisfaction
- Better grades in school
- Higher career success and job performance
- Higher lifetime income and savings

> *Empty your mind, be formless, shapeless – like water.*
>
> **-Bruce Lee**

HOW?

Use a time management system with four components:

1. Triage
2. Plan
3. Execute
4. Organize

Tips:

- Rigorously follow the system so you don't waste time wondering if you forgot something
- Check out the Maps for "Work Worth Doing" (page 75) and "Winning Strategy" (page 83)

You've got to think about the big things while you're doing small things, so that all the small things go in the right direction.

-**Alvin Toffler**

COMPONENT 1:
Triage

In medicine, triage is assessing the urgency of illnesses and deciding who gets treated first
- e.g., someone dying of a heart attack gets treated immediately and someone with a runny nose gets sent home

Triage all of your incoming actions by applying the 4 Ds:
- Delete
  - Be selective about accepting actions—your default should be "no"
    - According to the Pareto Principle (also known as the 80/20 Rule), 80% of your results come from 20% of your actions
      - These are the high-value actions worth your time
        - e.g., check out the Map for "Daily Habits" (page 17)
      - Try to Delete or Delegate everything else
  - Examples:
    - Delete low-value emails and messages
    - Block people who waste your time
    - Say no to events that aren't essential or fun
- Delegate
  - Hand off an action if it's not important for you to do it
- Do
  - If an action takes less than 2 minutes, do it now

- Defer
    - Some actions require more time or reflection
    - Write these actions down in a master list and post it in a visible place
        - e.g., a Word document on your computer desktop or your smartphone home screen
    - When you have time, Plan and Execute these actions

Tips:
- Triage your incoming actions at convenient times for you
    - e.g., check your email at the beginning and end of the day
- Don't let people interrupt your day unless it's extremely urgent
    - Turn off alerts and notifications on your smartphone and computer
    - Explain to your manager and co-workers that you work best if you're not constantly interrupted
        - Schedule times to review actions with them
- If an important thought arises in your mind, write it down immediately
    - This keeps your mind open for new thoughts
- The mind can hold a maximum of 3-4 items at a time (the ideal is 1)

The difference between successful people and really successful people is that really successful people say "no" to almost everything.

-Warren Buffett

Nothing is so fatiguing as the eternal nagging of an uncompleted task.

-William James

COMPONENT 2:
Plan

For Deferred actions, plan steps and write a list
- Each step should include specific information
    - e.g., book a doctor's appointment for Wednesday at 10am by calling (123) 456-7890
- As you finish steps, cross them off the list
    - This way, it's easy to resume steps if you don't finish everything at once

In your calendar, schedule time to do steps and set up alerts before major deadlines
- e.g., if you're giving a speech in 4 weeks, set a deadline for a first draft in 2 weeks

Tips:
- Prioritize actions by scheduling important ones sooner and allocating more time
    - If you report to a manager, regularly review priorities and progress so you don't get overwhelmed with actions
- For more complex actions, consider creating a Gantt chart with major steps and deadlines
- Update your calendar immediately with new meetings, appointments, and special dates
    - e.g., dentist appointments, birthdays
    - e.g., tax filing date, registration dates, bill payment dates
- When you Delegate an important action, consider sending a briefing note that includes the goal, suggested plan and schedule, and check-in times

The Five Ps: Prior Planning Prevents Poor Performance.
-**United States Marine Corps**

Goals are dreams with deadlines.
-**Diana Scharf Hunt**

COMPONENT 3:
Execute

When you work on actions, remember the following guidelines:
- Focus on one thing at a time
  - Multi-tasking causes poorer performance
  - It takes time and mental effort to switch your attention
- Prevent distractions
  - e.g., close your office door and turn off your phone
  - e.g., block out ambient noise by wearing earphones and listening to the same song on repeat

Tips:
- At the beginning of each day, set alarms on your smartphone that tell you when to prepare or leave for your next meeting
  - e.g., most alarms can be set for 5 minutes before your meeting
  - This way, you can focus completely on your work and not worry about missing a meeting

The secret of getting ahead is getting started. The secret of getting started is breaking your complex overwhelming tasks into small manageable tasks, and then starting on the first one.
-**Mark Twain**

> *You must be slow in deliberation and swift in execution.*
>
> -Napoleon Bonaparte

COMPONENT 4:
Organize

Create a filing system on your computer to organize your actions and documents

- Each major action should have its own folder
    - e.g., a finance folder with sub folders for your bank statements, credit card invoices, utility bills, income tax documents, etc.

Create sub folders for each year

- Each document should have a date for easy reference
    - e.g., "credit card invoice 20160906"
    - Store older versions of the same document in a sub folder

Create a password-protected master document to store your passwords and important information.

Tips:

- Store documents in digital form when possible
    - e.g., paperless invoices
    - e.g., scan paper documents or take photos with your phone
- Schedule regular backups of your computer and store the backups in different locations

> *For every minute spent organizing, an hour is earned.*
>
> -Benjamin Franklin

Suggested reading

- *Getting Things Done: The Art of Stress-Free Productivity* by David Allen

Next steps

You now have a proven system for freeing your time. But what happens when you encounter a problem that consumes your time? The next Map will show you how to solve the hardest problems faster.

MAP 4

Creative Problem Solving

*I*magine what your life would be like if there were no books. No newspapers or public libraries. Instead, you get your news from a man on the street corner. You learn about far-off lands from the travelers at the pub. You are taught history by the old woman who knits by the fire.

This was what it was like in the Middle Ages. Few families could read and even fewer could afford books. Books were expensive and rare because scribes had to painstakingly copy each page by hand. In 1440, everything changed. Suddenly, books were mass produced and prices dropped dramatically. Now even the poorest people could buy books, learn to read, and expand their minds.

What happened? Johannes Gutenberg invented the first printing press in Europe. He combined the movable type of coin punches and the power of mechanized wine presses. By connecting two seemingly unrelated things, Gutenberg dramatically improved the lives of millions of people and changed the course of history.

Creativity is the act of taking existing things and combining them into new ones. Why does creativity matter when it comes to problem solving? Because there is a solution to just about every problem if you can find and rearrange the right building blocks. This Map will teach you how.

Creativity is just connecting things. When you ask creative people how they did something, they feel a little guilty because they didn't really do it, they just saw something. It seemed obvious to them after a while. That's because they were able to connect experiences they've had and synthesize new things. And the reason they were able to do that was that they've had more experiences or they have thought more about their experiences than other people.

-**Steve Jobs**

WHY?

You can achieve your goals faster and better with creative solutions.

You can improve your creative problem solving with a proven system.

HOW?

There are five parts to the creative problem-solving system:

1. Identify the right problem
2. Prepare your knowledge
3. Generate lots of solutions
4. Incubate the problem
5. Test your solution

PART 1:
Identify the right problem

Sometimes it's hard to know if you're solving the true problem or only a symptom of the problem

- Ask yourself "5 Whys" to get to the root of a problem

Example problem: I'm not exercising enough

1. Q: Why are you not exercising enough?
   A: I don't have enough time

2. Q: Why don't you have enough time?
   A: I have too many tasks to do every day

3. Q: Why do you have too many tasks to do every day?
   A: I have trouble saying no

4. Q: Why do you have trouble saying no?
   A: I don't want to disappoint people

5. Q: Why don't you want to disappoint people?
   A: I want people to like me

> *If I had an hour to solve a problem I'd spend 55 minutes thinking about the problem and 5 minutes thinking about solutions.*
>
> **-Albert Einstein**

> *It isn't that they can't see the solution. It's that they can't see the problem.*
>
> **-G.K. Chesterton**

PART 2:
Prepare your knowledge

Creativity is easier if you have lots of raw materials to combine into new solutions

- Prepare your mind by learning about the problem
- It also helps if you've accumulated a lot of general knowledge
    - e.g., one of the "Daily Habits" (page 17) is to read for 30 minutes every day

Creativity is also easier if you can draw on diverse skills
- e.g., Nobel Prize winners are more likely to have hobbies like arts and crafts
- Consider learning an art like music, painting, or writing

The only art I'll ever study is stuff that I can steal from.
-David Bowie

What you need is a latticework of mental models in your head. And you hang your actual experience and your vicarious experience (that you get from reading and so forth) on this latticework of powerful models. And, with that system, things gradually get to fit together in a way that enhances cognition. And you need the models—not just from one or two disciplines, but from all the important disciplines. You need the best 100 or so models from microeconomics, physiology, psychology particularly, elementary mathematics, hard science and engineering. You don't have to be a huge expert in any of those fields. All you've got to do is take the really big ideas and learn them early and well.
-Charlie Munger

PART 3:
Generate lots of solutions

The more solutions you generate, the better your chances of creating a great one.

Here are some techniques:
- Ask yourself questions that make you take a different perspective
    - e.g., how would you solve the problem if you had unlimited time, money, and resources?
    - e.g., in an ideal world, what would the solution look like?
- Think of crazy and unusual solutions—don't censor yourself
- Try associating ideas and concepts from different fields
    - e.g., are there principles from history or art that might apply?
- Visualize the problem intensely in your imagination
    - e.g., Albert Einstein imagined himself riding alongside a beam of light to discover the Special Theory of Relativity

The best way to have a good idea is to have a lot of ideas.
-Linus Pauling

For every good idea, ten thousand idiotic ones must first be posed, sifted, sniffed, tried, and discarded. A mind that's afraid to toy with the ridiculous will never come up with the brilliantly original.
-David Brin

PART 4:
Incubate the problem

Your subconscious mind can often discover better solutions than your conscious mind.

Here are some methods for your subconscious mind to incubate the problem:
- Take a break and do something relaxing
    - e.g., go for a walk or listen to music

- Keep your mind clear and in the present
    - e.g., meditation is one of the "Daily Habits" (page 17)
- Sleep on the problem

The intuitive mind is a sacred gift and the rational mind is a faithful servant. We have created a society that honors the servant and has forgotten the gift.

-Albert Einstein

The test of a first rate intelligence is to hold two ideas in our mind at the same time and still retain the capacity to function. You must, for example, be able to see that things are hopeless, yet be determined to make them otherwise.

-F. Scott Fitzgerald

PART 5:
Test your solution

Once you've developed a solution to your problem, test it in reality and see if it works.

If not, repeat the system and try again.

Suggested reading
- *Steal Like an Artist* by Austin Kleon
- *Einstein: His Life & Universe* by Walter Isaacson

Next steps

Creative problem solving is one of the most valuable systems you can learn. The next Map applies this system to a common problem: how to become financially free so you can work on whatever you want.

MAP 5

Financial Freedom

At 21, Pete Adeney mapped out his dream life. The steps were: graduate from college, earn good money as a software engineer, buy a nice house and car, buy a beach house for weekends, work his way up to CEO.

One year later, Pete's plan was on track. He graduated, landed a well-paid job at a software company, and bought a second-hand sports car. He ate at trendy restaurants and vacationed at beach resorts. Soon he would have everything he desired, just like the top executives at the company.

Two more years passed and Pete's plan was still on track. But he started noticing his best-paid colleagues were paying a high price for their money. They were stressed out and constantly distracted. They owned big houses and cottages but didn't have time to enjoy them. They had to make more and more money to finance fancier and fancier lifestyles.

By 24, Pete realized what he truly wanted was freedom. Freedom to play with his kids. Freedom to read books. Freedom to work on meaningful projects even if he wasn't being paid. With this new goal in mind, Pete created a new plan.

It only took 6 years. At 30, Pete retired. He had saved enough money that he could live off the interest for the rest of his life. And now that he was retired, he could work on whatever he wanted. For fun, he created a blog called *Mr. Money Mustache* to teach everyone how to become financially free. Within a few years, millions of people were reading his blog . . . which generated hundreds of thousands of dollars of extra income he didn't even need.

Imagine if you could be like Pete and retire in a few years. Then you could invest your time in changing the world. This module will show you the Map for financial freedom.

GOAL

Become financially free as fast as possible.

WHY?

Once you're financially free, you can work on making a difference without worrying about paying your bills.

Scientifically-proven benefits of being rich:

- Better health and longer life
- Less stress
- More happiness and life satisfaction

> *I had considerable passion to get rich. Not because I wanted Ferraris—I wanted the independence.*
>
> **-Charlie Munger**

HOW?

Save $500,000 as fast as possible

- $500,000 X 5% investment returns/year = $25,000 per year in passive cash flow = financial freedom

Part One: Save more money

1. Live on less than $25,000/year
2. Pay off all debts
3. Save $50,000 in cash

Part Two: Invest your savings

1. Invest 50% in Vanguard's S&P 500 Index fund
2. Invest the other 50% in Berkshire Hathaway stock

Part Three: Earn more money with a side business

1. Start a business that brings an existing product or service to a new market of users
2. Launch your business with a Minimum Viable Product (MVP)
3. Get 1,000 true fans to pay you $200 each year
4. Implement processes so the business can run without you

Warning: Being rich has disadvantages

Scientifically-proven risks of being rich:

- More likely to lie, cheat, and do unethical things because of loss of touch with humanity and reality
- Less charitable and less compassionate
- Less enjoyment of life's small pleasures
- Children have a higher risk of using drugs, anxiety, and depression because of achievement pressures and lack of quality time with busy parents

Now that you know these risks, you can take steps to counteract them

- e.g., meditation will help you notice people and appreciate things in the present

PART ONE:
Save more money

1. Live on less than $25,000/year

WHY?

$25,000/year in expenses allows you to live well in the present and save money for the future.

HOW?

Here is a budget for living well on $25,000/year:

Expense	Monthly Cost	Annual Cost
Rent	$ 1,000	$12, 000
Food	$ 360 ($12/day)	$ 4,320
Entertainment, restaurants, vacations	$ 200	$ 2,400
Clothing, other purchases	$ 200	$ 2,400
Transit pass	$ 150	$ 1,800
Internet	$ 40	$ 480
Cell phone	$ 40	$ 480
TOTAL	$ 1,940	$ 23, 880

A shortcut to riches is to subtract from our desires.

-Petrarch

Example: Cost of meals

Breakfast

- Oatmeal + peanut butter + sliced banana
- Cost: $0.40/meal
- 1 kg oatmeal = $2 = 40 meals at $0.05/meal
- 1 kg peanut butter = $3 = 30 meals at $0.10/meal
- 1 banana = $0.25

Lunch and Dinner

- Roast chicken + baby spinach + grape tomatoes
- Cost: $3.75/meal
- 1 pre-cooked roast chicken = $11 = 4 meals at $2.75/meal
- 454 g of pre-washed baby spinach = $5 = 7 meals at $0.71/meal
- 1 pint of grape tomatoes = $2 = 7 meals at $0.29/meal

Example: Saving $500,000

Here is how fast you can reach $500,000 for someone living in Ontario, Canada (you can use an online tax calculator for your province or state to determine your after-tax income).

Salary	After-tax income	Expenses	Savings	Time to reach $500,000
$35,000	$30,000	$25,000	$5,000	100 years
$50,000	$41,500	$25,000	$16,500	31 years
$100,000	$75,000	$25,000	$50,000	10 years
$150,000	$103,000	$25,000	$78,000	7 years

If you make a good income each year and spend it all, you are not getting wealthier. You are just living high. Wealth is what you accumulate, not what you spend.

-Thomas J. Stanley, *The Millionaire Next Door*

2: Pay off all debts

WHY?

You'll save money faster if you're not paying interest on debt.

Interest has three particularly bad consequences:
- Interest compounds, which means you'll end up paying back much more than your original loan
    - e.g., if you have a $100,000 loan at an interest rate of 7.5%, and you pay back $789 per month for 25 years, you'll end up paying back $221,697 ($100,000 for the original loan and $121,697 in interest)
- Interest is paid with after-tax dollars
    - e.g., you have to earn $1.30 in salary to pay back $1 in interest (because you have to pay $0.30 in taxes)

- Most debt has an interest rate that is higher than your expected investment returns
  - e.g., if your investment return is 8%/year and your credit card interest rate is 20%/year, then you'd be smarter to pay off your credit card than to invest

People can't do anything entrepreneurial or innovative or even nonprofit—anything that's not safe and well-paying—because they have this mountain of debt.

-Peter Thiel

3: Save $50,000 in cash

WHY?

It's a rainy day fund that protects you against unexpected bad luck

- e.g., imagine you lose your job and it takes you 2 years to find another one: $50,000 equals 2 years of living expenses

It lets you take advantage of deals and discounts

- e.g., you can stock up when there's a 50% discount
- e.g., you can offer to pay cash and see if the merchant will give you a discount in exchange for not paying a credit card processing fee
- If you're patient and wait for the right opportunities, the percentage savings should be much higher than the return on your investments

Once you have $50,000 in cash, then you can start investing your savings above this amount.

Example

In Florida, 14-year-old Willow Tufano was saving almost $500/month from selling used furniture and appliances on Craigslist.

In 2012, she used her savings to buy a house at auction for $12,000 (down from $100,000 at the peak of the real estate bubble) and rented it out for $8,400/year.

Willow was able to jump on this deal thanks to her savings, and now she has an asset that is generating positive cash flow every year and is likely to rise significantly in value over time.

> *An investor should act as though he had a lifetime decision card with just twenty punches on it.*
>
> -Warren Buffett

PART TWO:
Invest your savings

1. Invest 50% in Vanguard's S&P 500 Index fund

WHY?

This is a high-probability low-risk way to generate investment returns of 6% or more over the long term.

The S&P 500 Index tracks the performance of the 500 largest companies in the US

- This diversification means you're not exposed to the risk of owning only a few stocks

Vanguard has the lowest expense ratio of the major index funds

- e.g., Vanguard's S&P 500 Index has a Management Expense Ratio (MER) of 0.05%, which is almost half of the 0.09% MER of the SPDR S&P 500 Index (the most popular index in the US)

Vanguard has outperformed over 85% of actively-managed funds over the long term

- A major reason is much lower fees
    - e.g., actively-managed funds typically have MERs that are 20X higher than Vanguard

HOW?

Open a stock trading account with a low-cost discount brokerage

- For Americans, a good choice is TD Ameritrade
    - $9.99 per trade
    - $0 account minimum
    - No annual fees
- For Canadians, a good choice is Questrade
    - $4.95 per trade
    - $1,000 account minimum
    - $79.80 annual fee if balance < $5,000

Twice a year, invest 50% of your savings in shares of Vanguard's S&P 500 Index Exchange-Traded Fund (ETF)

- For Americans, the ETF ticker symbol is VOO
- For Canadians, the ETF ticker symbol is VSP

> *A low-cost index fund is the most sensible equity investment for the great majority of investors.*
>
> **-Warren Buffett**

2. Invest the other 50% in Berkshire Hathaway stock

WHY?

This is a high-probability low-risk investment that is likely to return 10% or more over the long term

- e.g., from 1965-2015, Berkshire Hathaway stock gained an average of 20.8% each year vs. 9.7% for the S&P 500 Index i.e., 11.1% outperformance each year
- Berkshire's market capitalization is $390 billion, which means it is unlikely to continue gaining 20.8% per year, but 10% seems quite possible

Berkshire has several large advantages that make it likely to continue this outperformance:

- Berkshire owns insurance companies that provide it with cost-free money in the form of insurance premiums that it can invest. Other companies usually have to pay for the cost of borrowing. This advantage probably accounts for 3-4% of the 11% in outperformance.
    - e.g., in 2015, Berkshire had $88 billion in insurance premiums to invest. 15% return = $13 billion. $13 billion divided by Berkshire's market capitalization of $390 billion = 3.4%.
- Berkshire is regularly offered incredible investment opportunities because it has over $70 billion in cash to invest and a sterling reputation thanks to its CEO and largest shareholder, Warren Buffett
    - e.g., in 2011 after the financial crisis, Berkshire invested $5 billion in Bank of America for 6% cumulative perpetual preferred stock (i.e., Berkshire gets paid $300 million in dividends every year) and also received the option to buy 700 million shares for $5 billion any time before September 2021 (this corresponded to a share price of $7.14; the current share price is $22, which means Berkshire already has a gain of $10 billion)
- Warren Buffett and his team have a 50-year track record of identifying companies that generate ever-increasing profits and waiting patiently to invest at a cheap price
- Berkshire is a mini-index fund of high-quality diversified companies that are likely to outperform the 500 companies in the index

- e.g., Berkshire owns more than 60 excellent companies and holds significant stakes in many more, including industry leaders such as American Express, Coca-Cola, Heinz, and Wells Fargo

HOW?

Twice a year, use your stock trading account to invest 50% of your savings in shares of Berkshire Hathaway Class B stock (Ticker symbol: BRK.B).

WHAT'S THE RISK TO BERKSHIRE'S PERFORMANCE WHEN WARREN BUFFETT DIES?

Warren Buffett is 89 years old.

His net worth is more than $70 billion and almost 99% of it is in Berkshire stock.

Buffett has implemented a system at Berkshire that is likely to ensure outperformance after he is gone, and he describes this system in pages 29-38 of Berkshire's 2014 Annual Report.

Nevertheless, there is always a risk that something unexpectedly bad could happen to Berkshire and that is why we recommend investing 50% of your savings in Berkshire and the other 50% in Vanguard's S&P 500 Index Fund.

Example: Faster financial freedom with investing

Over the long term, Vanguard's S&P 500 Index Fund should return 6% or more per year and Berkshire Hathaway should return 10% or more, which results in a combined return of 8% or more per year.

This compounded investment return of 8% will allow you to reach $500,000 in savings much faster than just savings alone:

Salary	After-tax income	Expenses	Savings	Time to reach $ 500,000	Time to reach $500,000 with 8% per year investment returns
$ 35,000	$ 30,000	$ 25,000	$ 5,000	100 years	28 years
$ 50,000	$ 41,500	$ 25,000	$ 16,500	31 years	16 years
$ 100,000	$ 75,000	$ 25,000	$ 50,000	10 years	8 years
$ 150,000	$ 103,000	$ 25,000	$ 78,000	7 years	6 years

Compounding is mankind's greatest invention because it allows for the reliable, systematic accumulation of wealth.

-Albert Einstein

PART THREE:
Earn more money with a side business

1. Start a business that brings an existing technology/product/service to a new market of users

WHY?
Harvard Business School professor Clayton Christensen found that this strategy increased the probability of creating a successful high-growth business from 6% to 37%

- Using an existing technology/product/service means you're minimizing your technical risk
- Targeting a new market of users means you aren't competing against established companies

A 37% chance of success still means there's a 63% chance of failure

- Reduce your risk by starting your new business on the side while

you work at your day job
- This approach has been shown to reduce risk of failure by an average of 33%

2. Launch your business with a Minimum Viable Product (MVP)

WHY?

An MVP is a product with just enough features that allows you to learn from your first customers and continue development. This approach gets you to market faster and avoids slow, expensive development of a product or features that customers don't actually want.

3. Get 1,000 true fans to pay you $200 each year

WHY?

A true fan is defined as a fan that will buy anything you produce.

1,000 true fans X $200 in sales/fan/year X 50% profit margin = $100,000 in profit = a successful business.

> *The single most important decision in evaluating a business is pricing power. If you've got the power to raise prices without losing business to a competitor, you've got a very good business. And if you have to have a prayer session before raising the price by 10 percent, then you've got a terrible business.*
>
> -Warren Buffett

4. Implement processes so the business can run without you

WHY?

It's easier to work on making a difference if you don't have to run your business at the same time.

HOW?

Think of your business as a franchise and create an operations manual of business systems and processes so others can be trained to run your business.

For more information, read *The E-Myth Revisited* by Michael E. Gerber.

> *With investing, best case you can return 10-20% consistently. Best, best, case. But if you start a business you can earn multiples of 10,000%.*
>
> -James Altucher

EXAMPLE: THIRD DOOR MARKETING

Think of your business as a franchise and create an operations manual of business systems and processes so others can be trained to run your business.

In 2020, I started a side business called Third Door Marketing. My start-up costs were less than $1,000 and I cleared $100,000 in profit in 12 months. Here is my business blueprint:

Social media service for companies:

Pricing:

3 social media posts per week

1 blog post per week

Includes copywriting, graphic design, and analytics

Monthly flat-rate fee of $1,000–2,000

Recurring revenues are ideal because you don't need to constantly find new customers

Notes:

- Create a virtual marketing agency with freelancers
    - Freelancers do the execution and this frees your time for client management, finding new customers, and your day job
    - You can pay a fair hourly wage, while still making a good profit on the monthly fee.
- To get your first customers, ask friends and family for referrals, then ask these people for referrals
- To lower your personal tax rate, consider paying yourself with dividends instead of salary

Cheap and easy online services for your business:

- To save lawyer fees, incorporate directly through the government
- Register a custom domain name with NameSilo
- Set up custom e-mail addresses with Google Workspace
- Design a logo with Canva (free) or Fiverr
- Create a custom website with Google Sites (free), Squarespace, Wix, or WordPress
- To save accounting fees, do your own bookkeeping with Wave (free), Xero, or QuickBooks

Suggested reading

- *The Innovator's Dilemma: When New Technologies Cause Great Firms to Fail* by Clayton Christensen
- *The Lean Startup: How Today's Entrepreneurs Use Continuous Innovation to Create Radically Successful Businesses* by Eric Ries

Next steps

Now you have a Map for setting yourself financially free. But what will you do with your freedom? The next Map will show you how to find work you love.

MAP 6

Love Your Work

It took 56 hours for Shawn Askinosie to travel halfway around the world from his home in Springfield, Missouri to the Tanzanian village of Mababu. Shawn was there to meet a group of cocoa farmers. When he arrived, students ran down the road to greet him. They clapped and sang, "We are happy! We are happy to be together!"

Shawn cried. The first time he had visited, the children had been starving because they could only afford one meal a day. Now, their faces were full and their eyes were hopeful for the future.

The change was thanks to Shawn's company Askinosie Chocolate. By buying cocoa beans directly from farmers and then hand-crafting them into premium products, Shawn's company was able pay 48% more money and dramatically improve the lives of the entire village. Oprah's magazine named Shawn as "One of 15 Guys Who Are Saving the World" and Forbes recognized Askinosie Chocolate as one of the "25 Best Small Companies in America."

12 years earlier, Shawn's life was completely different. He was a high-powered criminal lawyer who defended murderers and rapists. He hadn't lost a case in 20 years. But he was burnt out and depressed. Shawn tried different things to be happy, from buying a Mercedes to volunteering in a hospice. But nothing worked. Not even Googling "What should I do with my life?" Then one day, Shawn decided to make some chocolate. The first batches tasted terrible. But he kept

at it. The turning point was a 10-day trip to Ecuador, run by a master chocolatier from France. From that small beginning, Askinosie Chocolate was born.

It can be hard to find work you love. But Shawn's story points the way. You're looking for work that helps people, makes their lives better, brings them happiness. And it's work that you're good at or can become good at. Now that you know where you're going, this Map will help you get there faster.

WHY?

Scientifically-proven benefits of loving your work:

- You're more likely to work harder and this increases your likelihood of success
- Higher happiness

Scientifically-proven benefits of higher happiness:

- Higher income
- More good friends and social support
- Happier marriage
- Better health

> *I could force myself to be fairly good in a lot of things, but I couldn't be really good in anything where I didn't have an intense interest.*
>
> **-Charlie Munger**

> *Do what turns you on. Do something that if you had all the money in the world, you'd still be doing it. You've got to have a reason to jump out of bed in the morning. Don't look for the money. Look for something you love, and if you're good, the money will come.*
>
> **-Warren Buffett**

HOW?

To be happy, your work must fulfill three universal psychological needs:

1. Autonomy: control over your work and time
2. Competence: the ability to do something effectively
3. Relatedness: working with people you care about and who care about you too

Note that it takes years of deliberate practice and coaching to become an expert.

In addition, you'll be happier if your work reflects your true self

- i.e., your underlying feelings, values, and desires

To do the work you love, there are two main approaches:

1. Make your current job more fulfilling
    - This is possible even in lower-status jobs
        - e.g., a study found that 33% of administrative assistants felt their job was a calling
    - This is easier the more valuable you are to your employer
        - e.g., if you're a star employee, you're more likely to be allowed to set your own schedule
2. Find a new job that's more fulfilling
    - This is easier the less you need money
        - e.g., if you have financial freedom, you can prioritize a fulfilling job over a high-paying one
        - To make more money, you can start a business on the side
            - e.g., learn how with the Maps for "Financial Freedom" (page 53) and "Winning Strategy" (page 83)

The highest reward for a man's toil is not what he gets for it, but what he becomes.

-John Ruskin

> *Remembering that I'll be dead soon is the most important tool I've ever encountered to help me make the big choices in life. Because almost everything—all external expectations, all pride, all fear of embarrassment or failure—these things just fall away in the face of death, leaving only what is truly important.*
>
> -Steve Jobs

Warning: It can be difficult to know your true self

Your brain uses two systems for thinking and they function mostly independently:
- Conscious: slow, calculating, and logical
- Subconscious: fast, intuitive, and emotional

It's easy for your conscious mind to make choices without listening to your subconscious, especially when you're busy, stressed, or tired
- This is why getting a good night's sleep and meditating are part of the Map for "Daily Habits" (page 17)

When your conscious ignores your subconscious, this can make you think you're working on something you love but you actually don't
  - e.g., some doctors don't truly want to be doctors but they rationalize that they love their jobs because they're helping people

Here are some ways to get your conscious mind aligned with your subconscious and know your true feelings, values, and desires:
- Practice listening to your gut
  - i.e., ask yourself how you feel about something and notice the emotion that arises
- Meditate to increase your self-awareness
- Visualize yourself doing the work and observe the emotions you feel

- Schedule reflective time for self-examination
- Write stream of consciousness and then reflect on what you wrote

Follow your heart, but listen to your head.

-Steve Jobs

If you know the enemy and yourself, you need not fear a hundred battles. If you know yourself but not the enemy, for every victory you will also suffer a defeat. If you know neither the enemy nor yourself, you will succumb in every battle.

-Sun Tzu

Example:
Questionnaire for Eudaimonic Well-Being (QEWB)

Aristotle (384–322 BC) proposed that true happiness arises from *eudaimonia*, being true to one's *daimon* or inner self

- According to Aristotle, you should develop what is best within you and use your skills and talents in the service of humanity

Scientists have developed a questionnaire that can help you determine whether you love your work:

- I find I get intensely involved in many of the things I do each day
- I believe I have discovered who I really am
- My life is centered around a set of core beliefs that give meaning to my life
- It is more important that I really enjoy what I do than that other people are impressed by it
- I believe I know what my best potentials are and I try to develop them whenever possible
- I feel best when I'm doing something worth investing a great deal of effort in

- I can say that I have found my purpose in life
- I believe it is important to know how what I'm doing fits with purposes worth pursuing
- I usually know what I should do because some actions just feel right to me
- When I engage in activities that involve my best potentials, I have this sense of really being alive
- I find a lot of the things I do are personally expressive for me
- It is important to me that I feel fulfilled by the activities that I engage in
- I believe I know what I was meant to do in life

We don't make movies to make money, we make money to make more movies.

-Walt Disney

If your life were to end suddenly and unexpectedly tomorrow, would you be able to say you've been doing what you truly care about today?

-Randy Komisar

Warning: Not all work you love is worth doing

There are social causes and award-winning companies where people love their work and believe they're doing something great that contributes to humanity.

But it's often hard to identify the frauds because their marketing and messaging are so good

- e.g., In 1999, Enron was recognized by Fortune magazine as one of the "Best Companies to Work for in America" for reasons such as "women comprise nearly one-third of upper management"

and the company had "a matching charitable gift program of up to $15,000 per employee"
- In 2001, Enron went bankrupt after it was revealed that employees throughout the company were engaged in a massive accounting fraud

Half the work that is done in this world is to make things appear what they are not.

-E.R. Beadle

There are a lot of smart people and a lot of them cheat, so it's not easy to win.

-Charlie Munger

Suggested reading
- *The Artist's Way: A Spiritual Path to Higher Creativity* by Julia Cameron
- *A Return to Love: Reflections on the Principles of a Course in Miracles* by Marianne Williamson
- *Untamed* by Glennon Doyle

Next steps
It can be challenging to find work you love. And it's even more challenging to find work you love and which is truly worth doing. The next Map will help you assess the impact of your work.

MAP 7

Work Worth Doing

Almost everyone agrees that eradicating poverty in Africa is a worthy cause. Rich countries have donated more than $1 trillion over the last 60 years. Musicians write songs and hold benefit concerts. Researchers and economists publish books and give Ted Talks.

Despite this, children are still starving. Almost half the adult population is illiterate. Clean water is a luxury. People are dying from preventable diseases. Corrupt officials rule, often entrenched by the aid that was meant to help Africa's poor. The problem is it's hard to know which solutions are worthwhile and which ones have unintended consequences.

For example, which idea do you think has done more good for Africans: clothing donations or a for-profit noodle company? Most people would answer clothing donations. But they'd be wrong — 70% of donated clothes end up in Africa and have devastated local textile industries because they can't compete. In contrast, over the last 30 years, a noodle company called Indomie has provided low-cost meals to billions of people. They also generated thousands of jobs, built important distribution infrastructure, and created a $1-billion-dollar market that bolsters the African economy.

How can you make sure that your work will actually make the world a better place? This Map will show you how to test your world-changing idea so you can do work that is truly worth doing.

GOAL

Do work that is truly worth doing.

WHY?

Almost everyone wants to do work that makes the world a better place, but not all work really matters and some work has tragic consequences.

HOW?

Here are three suggestions:

1. Solve the root problem, not symptoms
2. Listen to smart people who disagree with you
3. Run small experiments and invest in success

> *The secret of the truly successful, I believe, is that they learned very early in life how not to be busy. They saw through that adage, repeated to me so often in childhood, that anything worth doing is worth doing well. The truth is, many things are worth doing only in the most slovenly, halfhearted fashion possible, and many other things are not worth doing at all.*
>
> **-Barbara Ehrenreich**

SUGGESTION 1:
Solve the root problem, not symptoms

It is easy to go from crisis to crisis without solving the underlying problem

- e.g., there are 233 million desperately hungry people in Africa

- o Famine relief shipments and celebrity aid concerts address the immediate need
- o But solving the underlying problem requires decades of boring, behind-the-scenes investment in African farmers, local marketplaces, and indigenous crops

Check whether you're working on the root problem by working backwards from the ideal world where you're not limited by time, money, or other resources

- e.g., in the ideal world, there would be no racism

Then figure out the first small step from your current situation towards the ideal world

- e.g., let's start by reducing racism in my classroom
    - o Check out the Map for "Creative Problem Solving" (page 47) to invent solutions that get you to the ideal world faster

Imagine a world in which every single person on the planet is given free access to the sum of all human knowledge.
-Jimmy Wales, founder of Wikipedia

Begin with the End in Mind means to begin each day, task, or project with a clear vision of your desired direction and destination, and then continue by flexing your proactive muscles to make things happen.
-Stephen R. Covey

SUGGESTION 2:
Listen to smart people who disagree with you

Confirmation bias is when you favor information that confirms your existing belief

- It makes it hard for you to assess your work objectively, especially if you've invested time, effort, and emotions

Here are two ways to counter your natural bias:

1. Deliberately seek out smart people who disagree with you, and then deeply understand their arguments
2. Ask yourself questions such as:
    - What bad things could happen from my work?
    - How could someone use my work to harm others?

> *I never allow myself to have an opinion on anything that I don't know the other side's argument better than they do.*
>
> **-Charlie Munger**

> *It is the mark of an educated mind to be able to entertain a thought without accepting it.*
>
> **-Aristotle**

Example: Increasing minimum wage

Imagine you are the mayor of a city and you want to increase the minimum wage to $15/hour to reduce poverty.

You seek out an opposing councilor and she says, "Other states have increased the minimum wage and this caused small businesses to close and people to lose their jobs. Your plan will make things worse for our city's poorest people."

Then you ask how someone could harm others with the rise in minimum wage?

- One possibility is some business owners may use it as an excuse to lay off workers and replace them with self-serve kiosks

Overall, these opposing viewpoints can balance your enthusiasm with caution, and provide early warnings if you still decide to go ahead.

> *A minimum wage law is, in reality, a law that makes it illegal for an employer to hire a person with limited skills.*
> **-Milton Friedman**

SUGGESTION 3:
Run small experiments and invest in success

Even if you're working on a root problem and you've considered opposing viewpoints, your best-laid plan may still have unforeseen consequences.

Reduce this risk by running small experiments with this process:

1. Create a Minimum Viable Product (MVP)
    - An MVP is a product or service with just enough features to satisfy early customers, and provides feedback for future development
2. Test your MVP in the real world with a small group of representative users
    - Assess the impact of your MVP with hard-to-game metrics
        - e.g., did your work make people significantly happier, wealthier, healthier, or smarter?

3. Show your data
    - Show your results to your smartest critic to counter confirmation bias
4. If the first 3 steps are positive, scale up to larger and larger groups

No plan survives contact with the enemy.
                                            -Helmuth von Moltke the Elder

Prediction is very difficult, especially if it's about the future.
                                            -Niels Bohr

NOTE: Improve your odds with worldly wisdom

Charlie Munger is a spectacularly successful investor and partner of Warren Buffett at Berkshire Hathaway Inc.

Munger suggests that you can consistently make better decisions by using a "latticework" of mental models that draw from major disciplines such as psychology, history, mathematics, physics, biology, and economics

- This "worldly wisdom" can help you identify work worth doing and predict opportunities and problems before they arise

What is elementary, worldly wisdom? Well, the first rule is that you can't really know anything if you just remember isolated facts and try and bang 'em back. If the facts don't hang together on a latticework of theory, you don't have them in a usable form. You've got to have models in your head. And you've got to array your experience both vicarious and direct on this latticework of models.
                                            -Charlie Munger

I suppose it is tempting, if the only tool you have is a hammer, to treat everything as if it were a nail.

-Abraham Maslow

Suggested reading
- *The Great Mental Models Volume 1: General Thinking Concepts* by Shane Parrish and Rhiannon Beaubien
- *Seeking Wisdom: From Darwin to Munger* by Peter Bevelin
- *Poor Charlie's Almanack: The Wit & Wisdom of Charles T. Munger* by Charlie Munger
- *The Prosperity Paradox* by Clayton Christensen

Next steps

You've found work you love and you think it will truly make the world a better place. What do you need next? An amazing plan to make your dream a reality. The next Map will help you create your world-changing strategy.

MAP 8
Winning Strategy

It is the year 207 AD in ancient China. A hermit lives peacefully in his thatched cottage on a mountainside. He is reading when he hears a knock at the door. It is a warrior named Liu Bei and he wants to know how to defeat a tyrant and restore prosperity to the Han Dynasty.

The hermit's name is Zhuge Liang and he will become famous as one of the greatest military geniuses of all time. He will lead Liu Bei and his son to victory. He will become prime minister of the new state. His wisdom will be chronicled in an epic work of Chinese literature called *Romance of the Three Kingdoms*. How will a hermit accomplish so much? The answer is superior strategy.

In one campaign, Zhuge Liang is tasked with creating 100,000 arrows in 10 days. If he fails, he will be executed. It is an impossible mission. Even if his soldiers work day and night, they cannot succeed.

Undaunted, Zhuge Liang decides to use a different strategy. He builds 20 boats, each staffed with a few sailors and dozens of straw dummies. During a thick fog, he sails his boats towards the enemy's camp. His sailors beat their war drums and shout military orders. The enemy panics, convinced they are about to be attacked by thousands of soldiers. They launch volley after volley of arrows at the terrifying noise. The sailors take cover and the arrows strike only straw.

Three days later, Zhuge Liang returns to harbor with his boats and sailors unharmed. The enemy has lost 100,000 arrows and their morale. Zhuge Liang's superior strategy has won again.

With a winning strategy, the impossible becomes possible. This Map will help you craft your strategy so you can change the world as easily as possible.

GOAL

Achieve your "Work Worth Doing" as easily as possible.

HOW?

You need a great strategy.

This is important because you're probably fighting opponents who are bigger and stronger than you.

> *If you have the right strategy, you can make a lot of tactical errors and still be successful. If you have the wrong strategy, you can be a tactical genius and still be a failure.*
>
> **-Al Ries**

WHAT IS A GREAT STRATEGY?

A great strategy allows you to win without fighting. Here are three types of great strategies:

1. Avoid opponents
2. Take resources that your opponent doesn't care about
3. Defeat your opponent psychologically rather than physically

The second-best strategy is to fight indirectly rather than head-on.

> *The supreme art of war is to subdue the enemy without fighting.*
>
> **-Sun Tzu**

eBay is a shark in the ocean. We are a crocodile in the Yangtze River. If we fight in the ocean, we will lose. But if we fight in the river, we will win.

-Jack Ma, founder of Alibaba

WIN BY AVOIDING OPPONENTS

To win by avoiding opponents, social entrepreneurs can use the proven strategy of "new-market disruptive innovation"

- Harvard professor Clayton Christensen defines this as bringing an existing technology to a new market of users
    - By using an existing technology, there is no technical risk for research and development
    - By targeting new users, you gain the significant advantage of not having to change an entrenched system
        - Scientists have found that it is very difficult to change people's minds
        - One of the few effective ways is through peer pressure and social influence

It's very hard to change a system when the guy whose hand is on the switch benefits enormously and, perhaps, disproportionately from that system.

-Warren Buffett

There is nothing more difficult to carry out, nor more doubtful of success, nor more dangerous to handle, than to institute a new order of things.

-Machiavelli

EXAMPLES OF NEW-MARKET DISRUPTIVE INNOVATIONS

Grameen Bank brought microcredit loans to the rural poor in Bangladesh who previously did not have access to banking services.

With funding from the Bill & Melinda Gates Foundation, the Global Alliance for Vaccines and Immunization (GAVI) brought existing vaccines to children in developing countries who previously were unable to afford them.

WIN BY TAKING UNWANTED RESOURCES

You can do this by using the strategy of "low-end disruptive innovation"

- Clayton Christensen defines this as poaching your opponent's low-end customers by offering them a cheaper "good enough" product that is lacking features desired by high-end customers
    - Most opponents don't care about losing these unprofitable customers
- Over time, you can gradually improve your product and poach more customers, until eventually you drive your opponent out of the market

For more information on new-market and low-end disruptive innovations, read *The Innovator's Dilemma* by Clayton Christensen.

> *If you throw a frog in a pot of boiling water, it will hop right out. But if you put that frog in a pot of tepid water and slowly warm it, the frog doesn't figure out what's going on until it's too late. Boiled frog. It's just a matter of working by slow degrees.*
>
> -Stephenie Meyer

EXAMPLES OF LOW-END DISRUPTIVE INNOVATIONS

In 2006, Salman Khan started Khan Academy by posting free homemade educational videos on YouTube. Over time, Khan Academy kept improving the quality of their videos and they now serve millions of students.

The Aravind Eye Care System made cataract surgery affordable for millions of Indians using an "assembly line" system that is high volume and low cost. The all-in cost for an Aravind surgery is about $18 versus $1,800 in the United States. About 40% of patients pay for their surgeries and this subsidizes free surgeries for the other 60%.

> *In business we often find that the winning system goes almost ridiculously far in maximizing and/or minimizing one or a few variables—like the discount warehouses of Costco.*
>
> **-Charlie Munger**

WIN WITH PSYCHOLOGY

You can often win by using psychology against your opponents and getting them to defeat themselves.

One approach is to provoke and amplify their destructive emotions
- e.g., overconfidence and impatience can lead to careless mistakes
- e.g., pride can make them defend a losing position
- e.g., fear and anxiety can sap their will to fight
- e.g., greed and envy can lead to corruption

Another approach is to use psychology against your opponent's supporters and turn them against each other
- e.g., publicize your opponent's corruption and make their supporters distrustful and disgusted

- e.g., make your opponent so angry that they overreact unfairly, which causes public opinion to turn against them
    - Scientists have shown that human nature is hardwired to react strongly against unfairness

You can't overestimate the importance of psychology in chess, and as much as some players try to downplay it, I believe that winning requires a constant and strong psychology not just at the board but in every aspect of your life.

-**Garry Kasparov**

EXAMPLES OF WINNING WITH PSYCHOLOGY

In Tanzania, "sugar daddies" were infecting young women with HIV. In 2007, Johns Hopkins University launched a media campaign that ridiculed *fataki* (the Kiswahili slang term for sleazy old men). Sex with fataki became socially shameful and embarrassing. As a result, status-conscious young women turned down these relationships.

In 1930, Mohandas Gandhi wanted to free India from British rule. He accomplished this by targeting a widely-hated law that forced Indians to buy all of their salt from the government. In the "Salt March", Gandhi dramatically defied the unfair law in front of thousands of supporters. This simple act catalyzed non-violent protests across the country. The rule-enforcing bureaucrats responded with stricter laws, brutal beatings, and as many as 100,000 arrests. But this caused public opinion to turn against the government, and it was only a matter of time until the British were forced to withdraw.

Violent protests are less effective than non-violent ones because they trigger anger and fear in the brain, and these strong emotions drown out sympathy for unfairness.

Gandhi fervently promoted non-violence, but that didn't mean he was complacently accepting of the status quo. He resisted, but he did so without doing harm.

-The Dalai Lama

WIN BY FIGHTING INDIRECTLY

From 1800 to 1998, there were 170 wars around the world where one side had a military advantage of 5:1 or more. When the weaker side fought head-on, they won only 24 percent of the time. But when the weaker side fought indirectly and avoided their opponent's strengths, they won an astonishing 63 percent of the time.

- e.g., guerilla warfare is an indirect strategy in which small agile units attack an opponent's weakness, retreat to safety, and then repeat the attack on another weakness.
  - o Over time, the opponent usually gets frustrated and retaliates savagely. This angers allies and increases support for the guerillas.

You can adapt the principles of guerilla warfare to social entrepreneurship:

- Match your strengths against your opponent's weaknesses
  - o e.g., play up your underdog status in the media
  - o e.g., form autonomous cells that act faster than your opponent's slow-moving bureaucracy
- Retreat quickly and don't get pinned down
  - o e.g., avoid long and costly courtroom battles
- Provoke unfair overreactions that gain public sympathy

In guerrilla warfare, select the tactic of seeming to come from the east and attacking from the west; avoid the solid, attack the hollow; attack; withdraw; deliver a lightning blow, seek a lightning decision. When guerrillas engage a stronger enemy, they withdraw when he advances; harass him when he stops; strike him when he is weary; pursue him when he withdraws.

-Mao Zedong

Example: Affordable HIV drugs for South Africa

- In 1997, millions of poor black South Africans were dying of HIV/AIDS because big pharmaceutical companies refused to lower the prices of their life-savings drugs from $40/day to the $1/day it actually cost to manufacture them.
- To fight this injustice, President Nelson Mandela passed a law to break Big Pharma's patent monopoly and force them to offer drugs at reasonable prices.
- Big Pharma immediately filed a lawsuit to block the new law. They also spent millions on lobbyists and lawyers and enlisted the help of Vice President Al Gore and White House Chief of Staff John Podesta. Gore told Mandela to his face that the United States would not tolerate the legislation and threatened economic sanctions.
- Against these overwhelming odds, activist Jamie Love fought back. Over several years, he and his team enlisted support from 60 non-governmental organizations (NGOs) such as Health Action International and Médecins Sans Frontières.
- The NGOs publicized the ongoing AIDS deaths and relentlessly pressured Big Pharma and their supporters (Al Gore reversed his opposition after activists shamed his presidential campaign). By 2001, Big Pharma was sick of the public relations nightmare. They dropped their case against Mandela and South Africa. Love and his guerillas had won.

There are three types of people in this world: sheep, wolves, and sheepdogs. Some people prefer to believe that evil doesn't exist in the world, and if it ever darkened their doorstep, they wouldn't know how to protect themselves. Those are the sheep. Then you've got predators who use violence to prey on the weak. They're the wolves. And then there are those blessed with the gift of aggression, an overpowering need to protect the flock. These men are the rare breed who live to confront the wolf. They are the sheepdog.

-**Wayne Kyle,** *American Sniper*

Warning: Power corrupts

Great strategy leads to great success leads to great power.

But feeling powerful also leads to two psychological weaknesses, which lower your odds of future success and can be exploited by your opponents:

- Overconfidence
- Lack of empathy

Prevent this by periodically exposing yourself to powerlessness

- e.g., volunteer in a soup kitchen

Meditate daily and improve your ability to observe your thoughts and actions.

> *Power is always dangerous. Power attracts the worst and corrupts the best.*
>
> —**Edward Abbey**

> *It is a curious thing, Harry, but perhaps those who are best suited to power are those who have never sought it. Those who, like you, have leadership thrust upon them, and take up the mantle because they must, and find to their own surprise that they wear it well.*
>
> —**J.K. Rowling, *Harry Potter and the Deathly Hallows***

Suggested reading
- *The Art of War* by Sun Tzu
- *Ender's Game* by Orson Scott Card

Next steps

Now you have work you love, you know it's worth doing, and you have a great strategy. You're missing one thing – great people who can help you achieve your goals. The next Map will show you how to find and recruit an amazing team.

MAP 9

Assemble a Great Team

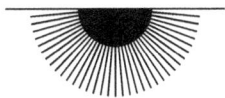

*I*magine you are sitting in the middle of a grand concert hall. The musicians file in, take their places, and ready their instruments. The conductor stands before them and raises his hands. The orchestra is about to begin.

You close your eyes and intricate harmonies of brass, string, and percussion wash over you. All of a sudden, something is wrong. You open your eyes and watch a violinist walk off the stage. Next, a cellist and a trumpeter abandon their stations. Musician after musician walks out until only the conductor remains, still waving his hands. The hall is silent.

The world's greatest composers know that it takes many instruments working in harmony to create a symphony. That's why they assemble great teams to execute their vision.

Like a composer, you need an amazing team to help you achieve your cause. This Map will show you how to attract, recruit, and keep your team.

GOAL

Assemble a great team to achieve your cause.

WHY?

Scientifically-proven benefits of working with a team:
- Faster and better problem solving
- More creative and innovative work

HOW?

Part One: Communicate a compelling vision

Part Two: Recruit the best team

Part Three: Be a great manager

> *No matter how brilliant your mind or strategy, if you're playing a solo game, you'll always lose out to a team.*
>
> **-Reid Hoffman**

> *When I meet successful people I ask 100 questions as to what they attribute their success to. It is usually the same: persistence, hard work, and hiring good people.*
>
> **-Kiana Tom**

PART ONE:
Communicate a compelling vision

WHY?

A compelling vision attracts the right people to your cause.

Scientifically-proven benefits of vision:
- Higher team performance
    - People are motivated to become the best version of themselves
- Greater team adaptability and openness
- Higher team creativity and innovation
- Lower team turnover

A vision is not just a picture of what could be; it is an appeal to our better selves, a call to become something more.
-**Rosabeth Moss Kanter**

He who has a why to live can bear almost any how.
-**Friedrich Nietzsche**

HOW?

Use lots of vision imagery

- e.g., Martin Luther King, Jr.'s "I have a dream" speech
  - "I have a dream that one day even the state of Mississippi, a state sweltering with the heat of injustice, sweltering with the heat of oppression, will be transformed into an oasis of freedom and justice."

Appeal strongly to emotions first and follow up with logical reasons

- It is especially powerful to appeal to negative emotions and then provide a specific solution
  - e.g., appeal to emotions such as fear of loss, anger, sadness, shame, guilt

Focus on one identifiable victim

- e.g., an emotional photo of a single child in need
- More than one victim leads to compassion fatigue and poor response

Make the vision easy to understand

- Choose a single familiar metaphor that frames your cause
  - An effective frame draws people into that way of thinking
    - e.g., "tax relief" is a frame that suggests we are being oppressed by taxes and need to be liberated from them
  - To learn more about effective framing, read *Pitch Anything* by Oren Klaff and *Ted Talks* by Chris Anderson

- Use simple words
    - Simple messages are perceived as more intelligent and truthful
        - e.g., Earthjustice: "Because the earth needs a good lawyer"

Make the vision easy to remember
- Rhymes seem more truthful and lead to more positive emotions
    - e.g., USDA Forest Service: "Give a hoot. Don't pollute."
- Alliteration is more memorable
    - e.g., EngAGE: "The art of active aging"

Think like a wise man but communicate in the language of the people.

-William Butler Yeats

If you can't explain it simply, you don't understand it well enough.

-Albert Einstein

If you want to change the world, change the metaphor.

-Joseph Campbell

Warning: With great persuasive power comes great responsibility
- The same persuasive techniques for crafting a compelling vision can be used for unethical purposes
    - e.g., pyramid scheme businesses reward people for persuading others to join
        - Newcomers are enticed with expectations of making easy money
        - Meanwhile, those at the top collect millions of dollars in residual commissions while those on the bottom struggle to recruit more people and sell the over-priced products

- Scientifically-proven risks of unethical company behavior:
  - Lower employee job satisfaction and higher turnover
  - Spread of corruption to other employees
  - Less customer trust and loyalty
  - Customers pay less money
- Before using persuasion, ask yourself the following questions:
  - Can you accomplish your goal without persuasion?
  - If you described your persuasion on the front page of the newspaper, would most people say you're being honest?
  - Will your persuasion result in a win for the other person?

Never do anything in life if you would be ashamed of seeing it printed on the front page of your hometown newspaper for your family and friends to see.

-Warren Buffett

PART TWO:
Recruit the best team

WHY?

Scientifically-proven benefits of recruiting people with the following qualities:

- Intelligence
  - Higher job performance
  - Greater leadership ability
  - Higher creativity
  - Faster learning
- Conscientiousness and grit
  - Higher job performance
  - Greater leadership ability

- - Higher perseverance
- Integrity
  - Higher job performance
  - Higher job satisfaction and lower turnover
- Emotional intelligence
  - Team is more comfortable being themselves and expressing themselves
    - This leads to faster learning and higher performance
  - Lower team turnover

What you really have to focus on is not trying to make ordinary people extraordinary. You need to hire extraordinary people.

-Phil Knight

One measure of leadership is the caliber of people who choose to follow you.

-Dennis A. Peer

In looking for people to hire, you look for three qualities: integrity, intelligence, and energy. And if they don't have the first, the other two will kill you.

-Warren Buffett

HOW DO I IDENTIFY PEOPLE WITH THESE QUALITIES?

INTELLIGENCE

Intelligence is the general capability for processing complex information.

Here are two ways to assess intelligence:
- Take the online version of the Wonderlic Cognitive Ability Test
    - You have 12 minutes to answer 50 multiple-choice questions
    - A score of 20 indicates average intelligence
    - The average score is 29 for engineers and programmers
- Ask the person to explain a complex topic in a simple way and then ask hypothetical questions to test the person's deep understanding
    - Note that knowledge is not the same thing as intelligence—you're looking for a person's ability to handle complex situations

Example of asking a person to explain a complex topic
- What is a topic you know well?
    - Cooking meat
- Tell me something about the topic that I wouldn't have guessed but I'll find interesting
    - Barbequed meat tastes great because of the Maillard reaction and caramelization
- Tell me about the Maillard reaction
    - It's a reaction that occurs between the amino acids in protein and the sugar in sauce or marinade when you heat meat at temperatures above 300°F

Examples of hypothetical questions:
- Would you get the Maillard reaction if you cooked the meat at very high heat? How about very low heat?
- Does the amount of fat influence the reaction?
- What happens if there is no sugar in the sauce?
- How could you cook meat without heat?

The difference between intelligence and education is this: intelligence will make you a good living.

-Charles F. Kettering

CONSCIOUSNESS AND GRIT

Conscientiousness is defined as the "tendency to be organized, responsible, and hardworking" and is related to grit, perseverance, delay of gratification, impulse control, ambition, and work ethic.

Here are some ways to assess it:
- Ask the person
    - How do you organize your day?
    - How do you organize your projects?
    - Would your friends and family say that you are always on time?
- Ask references and former colleagues
    - Is this person very organized?
    - Is this person very punctual?
- Give a small task and deadline
    - Please send me a 1-page essay on why our cause is important by 5pm on Friday

What is grit? Grit is refusing to give up. It's persistence. It's making your own luck.

-Peter Diamandis

INTEGRITY

It's easy for unethical people to fake being ethical and moral when you ask them questions.

A better way to assess integrity is to ask former colleagues how the

person would behave if given a lucrative but unethical opportunity
- e.g., would he lie to a customer if it meant he got a bonus of $20,000?

Good character is very efficient. If you can trust people, your systems can be way simpler. There's enormous efficiency in good character and dis-efficiency in bad character.
             -Charlie Munger

Nearly all men can stand adversity, but if you want to test a man's character, give him power.
             -Abraham Lincoln

EMOTIONAL INTELLIGENCE

The "Reading the Mind in the Eyes" test is a reliable way of assessing emotional intelligence
- It involves identifying the emotion shown in 36 photos of people's eyes
- The average score is 26.4 for women, 26.0 for men, and 21.9 for people with Asperger syndrome or high-functioning autism
- You can take the test online for free

No one cares how much you know, until they know how much you care.
             -Theodore Roosevelt

I've learned that people will forget what you said, people will forget what you did, but people will never forget how you made them feel.
             -Maya Angelou

PART THREE:
Be a great manager

WHY?

Scientifically-proven benefits of being a great manager:
- Higher team performance
- Higher team satisfaction and lower turnover
- Greater team commitment

> *No great manager or leader ever fell from heaven; it's learned, not inherited.*
>
> *-Tom Northup*

HOW?

Google has run hundreds of controlled experiments on its managers to determine the 8 best behaviors (most important first):

1. Be a good coach
    - Provide specific, constructive feedback, balancing the negative and the positive
    - Have regular one-on-ones, presenting solutions to problems tailored to your employees' specific strengths
2. Empower your team and don't micromanage
    - Balance giving freedom to your employees, while still being available for advice
    - Make "stretch" assignments to help the team tackle big problems
3. Express interest in team members' success and personal well-being
    - Get to know your employees as people, with lives outside of work
    - Make new members of your team feel welcome and ease their transition

4. Be productive and results-oriented
   - Focus on what employees want the team to achieve and how they can help achieve it
   - Help the team prioritize work and use seniority to remove roadblocks
5. Be a good communicator and listen to your team
   - Communication is two-way: you both listen and share information
   - Hold all-hands meetings and be straightforward about the messages and goals of the team, help the team connect the dots
   - Encourage open dialogue and listen to the issues and concerns of your employees
6. Help your employees with career development
   - Provide them with books about their interests
   - Introduce them to possible mentors
7. Have a clear vision and strategy for the team
   - Even in the midst of turmoil, keep the team focused on goals and strategy
   - Involve the team in setting and evolving the team's vision and making progress toward it
8. Have key technical skills so you can help advise the team
   - Roll up your sleeves and work side by side with the team, when needed
   - Understand the specific challenges of the work

A good manager is a man who isn't worried about his own career but rather the careers of those who work for him.

-H.S.M. Burns

The single biggest problem in communication is the illusion that it has taken place.

-George Bernard Shaw

Example of effective one-on-one meetings
- Schedule a weekly 30-minute update meeting with your team members
- Review the plan for the upcoming week
- Think of ways to help them solve problems and achieve their goals
- Schedule a monthly 60-minute assessment meeting and review these topics:
    - What were your priorities for the past 30 days? What progress did you make?
    - What are your priorities for the next 30 days?
    - What are we not doing that we should be doing?
    - What's the #1 problem at our company? Why?
    - Are you happy working here? Why?
    - What's not fun about working here?
    - How are you improving yourself?

The day the soldiers stop bringing you their problems is the day you stopped leading them. They have either lost confidence that you can help them or concluded that you do not care. Either case is a failure of leadership.

-Colin Powell

You are the same today that you are going to be in five years from now except for two things: the people with whom you associate and the books you read.

-Charles Jones

Suggested reading
- *Pitch Anything: An Innovative Method for Presenting, Persuading, and Winning the Deal* by Oren Klaff
- *TED Talks: The Official TED Guide to Public Speaking* by Chris Anderson
- *Work Rules!: Insights from Inside Google That Will Transform How You Live and Lead* by Laszlo Bock

Next steps

Read the Conclusion. Then start over.

Conclusion

BY RACHEL COLLIER

I once knew an old man who would ask me, "Imagine you're 80 years old and looking back on your life. What did you do that mattered? What made your life worth living?"

When I started writing this book, I would have answered that I solved a big problem, like eradicating world hunger or sexism. Now, I have a different answer.

When I'm 80 years old, I want to look back and see that I spent my life trying—trying to help people, trying to build better systems, and trying to act with real love every day.

Why has my answer changed? Because the truth is there is no perfect Map for solving the world's great injustices. There is too much indifference, too much chaos, and the battlefield transforms from moment to moment. This means there is really only one way to change the world: you must keep trying.

In the Introduction, I wrote that this book is magic. And it is. It's magic because I've tried my best to help you change the world. I could be wrong, but that's okay.

I'll keep trying.

Life is short. If you don't notice, it'll pass you by. That's why my head is in the clouds trying to pass the sky.

-Ludacris

We shall not cease from exploration. And the end of all our exploring will be to arrive where we started and know the place for the first time.

-T.S. Eliot

Feedback

Our goal for this book is to find the best people, stories, and systems for changing the world. If you have comments or feedback, please email us at *rachel.collier@thirddoor.ca*

References

LEARNING TO LEARN

AUTOMATIC ACTIONS WITHOUT CONSCIOUS THOUGHT

Libet B. (1981). The experimental evidence for subjective referral of a sensory experience backwards in time: reply to P. S. Churchland. *Philosophy of Science.* 48(2): 182–197.
- Reaction time is typically 0.25 seconds, but this slows down to 0.5-1.0 seconds with conscious thought

Flegal KE, Anderson MC. (2008). Overthinking skilled motor performance: or why those who teach can't do. *Psychon Bull Rev.* 15(5): 927–932.
- Consciously thinking about golf putting caused higher-skill golfers to drop their performance level to lower-skill golfers

Slingerland, Edward. (2014). *Trying not to try: The art and science of spontaneity.* Crown Publishers.
- Example of John McEnroe complimenting his opponents
- Spontaneous behavior is hard to fake, which means that spontaneous, unselfconscious people are unlikely to be fakers

Csikszentmihalyi M. (1990). *Flow: the psychology of optimal experience.* Harper & Row.

Miyamoto M. (2005). *The book of five rings: A classic text on the Japanese way of the sword* (T Cleary, Trans.). Shambhala. (Original work published 1644)

GET REAL-WORLD FEEDBACK

Yang C, Shanks DR. (2018). The forward testing effect: Interim testing enhances inductive learning. *J Exp Psychol Learn Mem Cogn.* 44(3): 485–492.
- Repeated testing improves retention of things you've already learned and also helps you learn new things

EVERYONE IS BIASED

Gazzaniga MS. (2013). Shifting gears: seeking new approaches for mind/brain mechanisms. *Annu Rev Psychol.* 64: 1–20.
- Experiments with split-brain patients revealed that there is a module in the left brain called the "Interpreter" that generates stories to explain why we act and feel the way we do
- It creates the personal narrative that gives you a sense of self

Dunning D et al. (2003). Why people fail to recognize their own incompetence. *Current Directions in Psychological Science.* 12(3): 83–87.
- People are unaware of their own incompetence because: (1) lack of skill prevents them from performing well, and (2) lack of expertise prevents them from realizing they are performing poorly
- e.g., poor performers scored in the bottom 12th percentile but estimated they were actually in the 60th percentile

Balcetis E, Dunning D. (2006). See what you want to see: motivational influences on visual perception. *J Pers Soc Psychol.* 91(4): 612–625.
- People's wishes and preferences influence what the visual system presents to conscious awareness

West RF, Meserve RJ, Stanovich KE. (2012). Cognitive sophistication does not attenuate the bias blind spot. *J Pers Soc Psychol.* 103(3): 506–519.
- Smart people think they are less biased than others, but on average they are actually more biased

GROWTH MINDSET AND CREATIVE OUTPUT

Burnette JL et al. (2013). Mind-sets matter: a meta-analytic review of implicit theories and self-regulation. *Psychol Bull.* 139(3): 655–701.
- People with mindsets "characterized by the belief that human attributes are malleable rather than fixed" were significantly more likely to engage in a number of goal-related behaviors and strategies linked to enhanced performance

Lazowski RA, Hulleman CS. (2016). Motivation interventions in education: A meta-analytic review. *Review of Educational Research.* 86(2): 602–640.
- Growth mindsets improve educational performance

Kaufman SB. (2015, December 29). Why creativity is a numbers game. *Scientific American.* Retrieved from https://blogs.scientificamerican.com/beautiful-minds/why-creativity-is-a-numbers-game/
- Creative geniuses immerse themselves in many diverse ideas and projects and they have extraordinary output
- The more ideas creators generate (regardless of the quality of each idea), the greater the chance they will produce a masterpiece

- e.g., Thomas Edison had roughly a one-third rejection rate for all the patents he led, and most of his 1,093 patents that were accepted were not commercially successful

Simonton DK. (1997). Creative productivity: A predictive and explanatory model of career trajectories and landmarks. *Psychological Review*. 104(1): 66-89.
- In fields as diverse as music, linguistics, chemistry, and geology, contributors in the upper 10% of lifetime output tended to produce about 50% of all the contributions to the field
- The "equal-odds rule" states that any particular work is just as likely to be a hit versus a failure. Therefore, the more works a person creates, the higher the likelihood that one of them will be a masterpiece.

10 YEARS OF DELIBERATE PRACTICE

Ericsson KA, Lehmann AC. (1996). Expert and exceptional performance: evidence of maximal adaptation to task constraints. *Annu Rev Psychol*. 47: 273-305.
- It takes about 10 years of preparation to attain an international level of skill
- Elite performers were able to exercise intensely for 4 hours/day for years without burning out

Ericsson KA, Krampe RT, Tesch-Roemer C. (1993). The role of deliberate practice in the acquisition of expert performance. *Psychological Review*. 100(3): 363-406.
- It takes 10 years of practice to become an expert in fields as diverse as music, mathematics, tennis, swimming, and long-distance running
- Coaches instruct individuals to engage in deliberate practice—activities that maximize improvement
- Rest and recovery after practices is important: top performers slept an average of 8.6 hours/day, napped an average of 2.8 hours/week, and spent 3.5 hours/day on leisure activities

Duke RA, Simmons AL, Cash CD. (2009). It's not how much; It's how: Characteristics of practice behavior and retention of performance skills. *Journal of Research in Music Education*. 56(4): 310-321.
- For pianists, total amount of practice time did not predict performance
- Instead, top-ranked pianists spent their practice time fixing errors

Stickgold R, James L, Hobson JA. (2000). Visual discrimination learning requires sleep after training. *Nat Neurosci*. 3(12): 1237-1238.
- Sleeping within 30 hours of training is required for improved performance

A backhanded complement: Roger Federer has turned his weakest shot into a weapon. (2017, April 5). *The Economist*.

Rosen S. (1981). The economics of superstars. *American Economic Review*. 71(5): 845-858.
- Tournament effect for superstars

Greenburg ZO. (2017, December 6). The world's highest-paid musicians of 2017. *Forbes*.
- Beyoncé earned $105 million in 2017

Bureau of Labor Statistics, U.S. Department of Labor. (2017). *Occupational Outlook Handbook, Musicians and Singers*. Retrieved from https://www.bls.gov/ooh/entertainment-and-sports/musicians-and-singers.htm
- Musicians and singers earned a median of $26.96/hour (corresponds to approximately $56,000 in full-time annual salary)

COACHING

Pennington B. (2014, January 9). Mikaela Shiffrin's swift, if unplanned, ascent to World Champion. *New York Times*.

Henry Ford. (n.d.). In *Wikipedia*. Retrieved June 11, 2018, from https://en.wikipedia.org/wiki/Henry_Ford

Henry Ford leaves Edison to start automobile company. (n.d.). In *History.com*. Retrieved July 23, 2020, from https://www.history.com/this-day-in-history/henry-ford-leaves-edison-to-start-automobile-company"

DAILY HABITS

Harrell E. (2015, October 30). How 1% performance improvements led to Olympic gold. *Harvard Business Review*. Retrieved from https://hbr.org/2015/10/how-1-performance-improvements-led-to-olympic-gold

Lem P. (2008). *Master life faster: How to be happy, health, wealthy, smart & social*.

HABITS

Baumeister RF, Vohs KD, Tice DM. (2007). The strength model of self-control. *Current Directions in Psychological Science*. 16(6): 351–355.
- Self-control is a limited resource and gets depleted as it is used

Vohs KD et al. (2008). Making choices impairs subsequent self-control: a limited-resource account of decision making, self-regulation, and active initiative. *J Pers Soc Psychol*. 94(5): 883–898.
- Making decisions depletes self-control

Nilsen P et al. (2012). Creatures of habit: accounting for the role of habit in implementation research on clinical behaviour change. *Implement Sci*. 7: 53.
- Habits involve cues, behaviors, and rewards that may be extrinsic or intrinsic

Wise RA. (2002). Brain reward circuitry: insights from unsensed incentives. *Neuron*. 36(2): 229–240.
- Rewards reinforce habits in the brain

Wood W, Witt MG, Tam L. (2005). Changing circumstances, disrupting habits. *J Pers Soc Psychol*. 88(6): 918–933.
- Changing the environment removed cues and disrupted habits

Kaushal N, Rhodes RE. (2015). Exercise habit formation in new gym members: a longitudinal study. *J Behav Med*. 38(4): 652–663.
- Exercising at least 4 times per week for 6 weeks was the minimum requirement to establish an exercise habit
- Predictors of habit formation were: consistently exercising, simple exercises that were easy to do, comfortableness of the exercise environment, and experiencing rewarding emotions for exercising

Lally P et al. (2010). How are habits formed: Modelling habit formation in the real world. *Eur J Soc Psychol*. 40: 998–1009.
- Participants performed an eating, drinking, or activity behavior every day for 12 weeks
- On average, it took 66 days for the behavior to become a habit, with a range between 18-254 days

1. EXERCISE FOR 30 MINUTES

Exercise guidelines

Garber CE et al. (2011). American College of Sports Medicine position stand. Quantity and quality of exercise for developing and maintaining cardiorespiratory, musculoskeletal, and neuromotor fitness in apparently healthy adults: guidance for prescribing exercise. *Med Sci Sports Exerc*. 43(7): 1334–1359.
- Aerobic exercise: At least 150 minutes of moderate-intensity exercise per week
    - e.g., 5 days/week of 30-60 minutes of moderate-intensity exercise
    - e.g., 3 days/week of 20-60 minutes of vigorous-intensity exercise
- Resistance exercise: Train each major muscle group 2-3 days each week
    - 2-4 sets with 8-12 reps improve strength and power
    - Wait at least 48 hours between training sessions
    - Flexibility exercise: At least 2-3 days each week to improve range of motion
    - Each stretch should be held for 10-30 seconds
    - Repeat each stretch 2-4 times
    - Neuromotor exercise: 2-3 days per week
    - e.g., tai chi, yoga

Aerobic training

Ross R et al. (2016). Importance of assessing cardiorespiratory fitness in clinical practice: A case for fitness as a clinical vital sign: A scientific statement from the American Heart Association. *Circulation*. 134(24): e653–e699.
- Cardiovascular fitness lowers risk of death, heart attack, stroke, heart failure, Alzheimer's disease, anxiety, depression, diabetes, and cancer

Lee D et al. (2014). Leisure-time running reduces all-cause and cardiovascular mortality risk. *J Am Coll Cardiol*. 64(5): 472–481.
- Running even 5-10 min/day and at slow speeds (<6 miles/hour) is associated with markedly reduce risks of death from all causes and cardiovascular disease

Gillen JB et al. (2016). Twelve weeks of sprint interval training improves indices of cardiometabolic health similar to traditional endurance training despite a five-fold lower exercise volume and time commitment. *PLoS One*. 11(4): e0154075.
- 5 minutes of sprint interval training (SIT) is equivalent to 45 minutes of moderate-intensity continuous training (MICT) as measured by peak oxygen uptake and insulin sensitivity
- SIT involves 3 sets of 20-second "all-out" cycle sprints interspersed with 2 minutes of slow cycling
- MICT involves 45 minutes of continuous cycling at 70% of maximum heart rate

Klika B, Jordan C. (2013). High-intensity circuit training using body weight: Maximum results with minimal investment. *ACSM Health Fit J*. 17(3): 8–13.
- High-intensity circuit training (HCIT) combines aerobic and resistance training into a single exercise circuit lasting 7 minutes
- Since bodyweight is used for resistance, the regimen can be performed anywhere
- Exercises are performed for 30 seconds with 10 seconds of transition time between exercises
- Jumping jacks, wall sit, push-up, abdominal crunch, step-up onto chair, squat, triceps dip on chair, plank, high knees/running in place, lunge, push-up and rotation, side plank

Resistance training

Melov S et al. (2007). Resistance exercise reverses aging in human skeletal muscle. *PLoS ONE*. 2(5): e465.
- Resistance training reverses aging in skeletal muscle

Morton RW et al. (2016). Neither load nor systemic hormones determine resistance training-mediated hypertrophy or strength gains in resistance-trained young men. *J Appl Physiol*. 121(1): 129–138.
- Lifting to failure builds maximal muscle
  - e.g., lots of repetitions of low weight or a few repetitions of high weight

Collier SR et al. (2010). Changes in arterial distensibility and flow-mediated dilation after acute resistance vs. aerobic exercise. *J Strength Cond Res*. 24(10): 2846-2852.
- Compared with aerobic exercise, resistance training increased blood flow to limbs and led to a longer-lasting drop in blood pressure after exercise

Moore DR et al. (2009). Ingested protein dose response of muscle and albumin protein synthesis after resistance exercise in young men. *Am J Clin Nutr*. 89(1): 161-168.
- Eating 20 grams of protein after exercise stimulates maximum muscle growth
- Neuromotor exercise for balance and coordination

Büssing A et al. (2012). Effects of yoga on mental and physical health: A short summary of reviews. *Evid Based Complement Alternat Med*. 2012: 165410.
- Yoga reduces anxiety and stress, and improves balance, flexibility, strength, weight loss, cardiovascular endurance, and back pain

Jahnke R et al. (2010). A comprehensive review of health benefits of qigong and tai chi. *Am J Health Promot*. 24(6): e1–e25.
- Tai chi improves bone health, lowers blood pressure, improves flexibility and balance, lowers anxiety and depression, and improves immune function

Healthier

Ekelund U et al. (2016). Does physical activity attenuate, or even eliminate, the detrimental association of sitting time with mortality? A harmonised meta-analysis of data from more than 1 million men and women. *Lancet*. 388(10051): 1302–1310.
- 60-75 minutes of moderate intensity exercise per day eliminates increased risk of death associated with high sitting time

Arem H et al. (2015). Leisure time physical activity and mortality: a detailed pooled analysis of the dose-response relationship. *JAMA Intern Med*. 175(6):959–967.
- Exercising for 30 minutes/day is associated with 30% lower mortality risk

Tworoger SS et al. (2003). Effects of a yearlong moderate-intensity exercise and a stretching intervention on sleep quality in postmenopausal women. *Sleep*. 26(7): 830-836.

Morning exercise improves sleep

Colberg SR et al. (2010). Exercise and Type 2 diabetes. *Diabetes Care*. 33(12): e147–e167.
- Exercise prevents Type 2 diabetes

Moore SC et al. (2016). Association of leisure-time physical activity with risk of 26 types of cancer in 1.44 million adults. *JAMA Intern Med*. 176(6): 816–825.
- Exercise reduces risk of 13 types of cancer

Wroblewski AP et al. (2011). Chronic exercise preserves lean muscle mass in masters athletes. *Phys Sportsmed*. 39(3): 172–178.
- Athletes aged 40-81 years who exercised 4-5 times/week did not experience age-related muscle loss

Khera AV et al. (2016). Genetic risk, adherence to a healthy lifestyle, and coronary disease. *N Engl J Med*. 375(24): 2349-2358.
- Even among patients with high genetic risk for heart disease, exercise and healthy diet reduced the risk by 50% compared with an unhealthy lifestyle

Puterman E et al. (2010). The power of exercise: buffering the effect of chronic stress on telomere length. *PLoS One*. 5(5): e10837.
- Exercise buffers effects of high stress on telomere length

Swift DL et al. (2014). The role of exercise and physical activity in weight loss and maintenance. *Prog Cardiovasc Dis*. 56(4): 441-447.
- Exercise has a small effect on weight loss and maintenance

Smarter

ten Brinke LF et al. (2015). Aerobic exercise increases hippocampal volume in older women with probable mild cognitive impairment: A 6-month randomized controlled trial. *Br J Sports Med*. 49(4): 248-254.
- 6 months of aerobic exercise improved spatial memory and hippocampal volume in older women

Villemure C et al. (2015). Neuroprotective effects of yoga practice: age-, experience-, and frequency-dependent plasticity. *Front Hum Neurosci*. 9: 281.
- Regular yoga practice countered age-related decrease in brain volume

Tolppanen AM et al. (2015). Leisure-time physical activity from mid- to late life, body mass index, and risk of dementia. *Alzheimers Dement*. 11(4): 434-443.e6.
- Participants who engaged in physical activity at least twice a week had a lower risk of dementia than those who were less active
- Becoming more physically active after midlife was shown to lower dementia risk

Alfini AJ et al. (2016). Hippocampal and cerebral blood flow after exercise cessation in master athletes. *Front Aging Neurosci*. 8: 184.
- Brain blood flow is significantly reduced when master athletes stop exercising for 10 days

Bolandzadeh N et al. (2015). Resistance training and white matter lesion progression in older women: Exploratory analysis of a 12-month randomized controlled trial. *J Am Geriatr Soc*. 63(10): 2052-2060.
- Resistance training significantly slowed progression of white matter lesions in older women

Gomez-Pinilla F, Hillman C. (2013). The influence of exercise on cognitive abilities. *Compr Physiol*. 3(1): 403-428.
- Exercise improves attention and cognitive processing speed

Oaten M, Cheng K. (2006). Longitudinal gains in self-regulation from regular physical exercise. *Br J Health Psychol.* 11(Pt 4): 717–733.
- Exercising 3-4 times per week for 2 months increased self-control across a variety of measures

Happier

Bartels M et al. (2012). Regular exercise, subjective wellbeing, and internalizing problems in adolescence: causality or genetic pleiotropy? *Front Genet.* 3: 4.
- Exercise causes happiness

Hogan CL, Mata J, Carstensen LL. (2013). Exercise holds immediate benefits for affect and cognition in younger and older adults. *Psychol Aging.* 28(2): 587–594.
- 15 minutes of aerobic exercise improves mood and memory

Mammen G, Faulkner G. (2013). Physical activity and the prevention of depression: a systematic review of prospective studies. *Am J Prev Med.* 45(5): 649–657.
- Exercise prevents depression

2. MEDITATE FOR 15 MINUTES

Lutz A et al. (2004). Long-term meditators self-induce high-amplitude gamma synchrony during mental practice. *Proc Natl Acad Sci USA.* 101(46): 16369–16373.
- Tibetan Buddhist monks who had performed 10,000 to 50,000 hours of compassion meditation had high-amplitude gamma activity that was the highest reported in the literature
- This type of brain activity is associated with moment-to-moment awareness and attention

Brewer JA et al. (2011). Meditation experience is associated with differences in default mode network activity and connectivity. *Proc Natl Acad Sci USA.* 108(50): 20254–20259.
- Meditation increases the brain networks involved in self-monitoring and cognitive control

Jha AP et al. (2015). Minds "At Attention": Mindfulness training curbs attentional lapses in military cohorts. *PLoS One.* 10(2): e0116889.
- An 8-hour 8-week program of mindfulness training significantly reduced attentional performance lapses in soldiers

Chambers R, Lo BCY, Allen NB. (2008). The impact of intensive mindfulness training on attentional control, cognitive style, and affect. *Cogn Ther Res.* 32: 303–322.
- 10 days of intensive mindfulness meditation training improved memory, attention, and mindfulness in novice meditators

Creswell JD et al. (2016). Alterations in resting-state functional connectivity link mindfulness meditation with reduced Interleukin-6: A randomized controlled trial. *Biol Psychiatry.* 80(1): 53–61.

- 3 days of mindfulness meditation training reduced interleukin-6 levels tested 4 months later (IL-6 is a biomarker of systemic inflammation)

Tang YY et al. (2007). Short-term meditation training improves attention and self-regulation. *Proc Natl Acad Sci USA*. 104(43): 17152–17156.
- 5 days of meditation practice improved attention and immune function and lowered stress, fatigue, and negative emotions

Goyal M et al. (2014). Meditation programs for psychological stress and well-being: a systematic review and meta-analysis. *JAMA Intern Med*. 174(3): 357–368.
- A review of 47 trials found that mindfulness meditation reduced anxiety, depression, and pain

Stanley EA et al. (2011). Mindfulness-based mind fitness training: A case study of a high-stress predeployment military cohort. *Cognitive and Behavioral Practice*. 18: 566–576.
- An 8-week program of mindfulness training decreased stress in U.S. Marines

3. WRITE 3 PAGES OF STREAM OF CONSCIOUSNESS

Smallwood J, School JW. (2014). The science of mind-wandering: Empirically navigating stream of consciousness. *Ann R Psychol*. 66:487-518

4. EAT A PALEO DIET OF PROTEIN, FAT, FRUITS, AND VEGETABLES

Paleolithic ancestors and hunter-gatherers

Jacobi R, Current A, Stringer C. (2000). Gough's Cave and Sun Hole Cave human stable isotope values indicate a high animal protein diet in the British Upper Palaeolithic. *J Archaeol Sci*. 27(1): 1–3.
- Paleolithic diets were high in animal protein as indicated by isotope ratios in bone collagen from skeletons

Cordain L et al. (2000). Plant-animal subsistence ratios and macronutrient energy estimations in worldwide hunter-gatherer diets. *Am J Clin Nutr*. 71(3): 682–692.
- Out of 229 hunter-gatherer societies, 73% derived >50% of their subsistence from hunted and fished animal foods
- No hunter-gatherer society is entirely or largely dependent (86-100% subsistence) on gathered plant foods, whereas 20% are highly or solely dependent (86-100%) on fished and hunted animal foods
- Excess consumption of dietary protein from the lean meats of wild animals leads to a condition referred to by early American explorers as "rabbit starvation", which initially results in nausea, then diarrhea, and then death
- Muscle tissue of wild hoofed animals typically contains 2-3% fat by weight
- Therefore, the solution of most hunter-gatherer societies to avoid excess

- dietary protein would likely have been an increase in total dietary fat from animal foods
  - The most plausible total energy from macronutrients for our hunter-gatherer ancestors would be 19-35% for protein, 22-40% for carbohydrate, and 28-58% for fat

Cordain L et al. (2005). Origins and evolution of the Western diet: Health implications for the 21st century. *Am J Clin Nutr.* 81(2): 341-354.
  - Dairy products, cereals, refined sugars, refined vegetable oils, and alcohol make up 72.1% of the total daily energy consumed by all people in the United States, and these types of foods would have contributed little or none of the energy in the typical pre-agricultural hominin diet
  - The widespread consumption of highly refined grain flours of uniformly small particulate size represents a recent secular phenomenon dating to the past 150-200 years
  - The dominant (>50% fat energy) fatty acids in the fat storage depots (adipocytes) of wild mammals are saturated fatty acids (SFAs), whereas the dominant fatty acids in muscle and all other organ tissues are polyunsaturated fatty acids (PUFAs) and monounsaturated fatty acids (MUFAs)
  - Because subcutaneous and abdominal body fat stores are depleted during most of the year in wild animals, PUFAs and MUFAs ordinarily constitute most of the total carcass fat
  - In the United States before 1850, virtually all cattle were free-range or pasture-fed and were typically slaughtered at 4-5 years of age
  - Modern feedlot operations involving as many as 100 000 cattle emerged in the 1950s and have developed to the point that a characteristically obese (30% body fat) 545-kg pound steer can be brought to slaughter in 14 months
  - Although 99% of all the beef consumed in the United States is now produced from grain-fed, feedlot cattle, virtually no beef was produced in this manner as recently as 200 years ago
  - Accordingly, cattle meat (muscle tissue) with a high absolute SFA content, low omega-3 fatty acid content, and high omega-6 fatty acid content represents a recent component of human diets
  - Within the past 20 years, substantial evidence has accumulated showing that long term consumption of high glycemic load carbohydrates can adversely affect metabolism and health
  - Milk, yogurt, and ice cream, despite having relatively low glycemic loads, are highly insulinotropic, with insulin indexes comparable with white bread
  - In the current US diet, the ratio of omega-6 to omega-3 PUFAs has risen to 10:1, whereas the ratio in hunter-gatherer diets predominant in wild animal foods has been estimated to be between 2:1 and 3:1

- Fresh fruit typically contains twice the amount of fiber in whole grains, and nonstarchy vegetables contain almost 8 times the amount of fiber in whole grains on an energy basis

Carrera-Bastos P et al. (2011). The western diet and lifestyle and diseases of civilization. *Res Rep Clin Cardiol.* 2: 15–35.
- Modern-day hunter gatherers have low blood pressure, excellent insulin sensitivity, BMI < 22 with no overweight or obese individuals, and better bone health

Kirchengast S. (1998). Weight status of adult !Kung San and Kavango people from northern Namibia. *Ann Hum Biol.* 25(6): 541–551.
- The !Kung San hunter-gatherer people have an average BMI of 19.1 for women and 19.4 for men

Pontzer H et al. (2012). Hunter-gatherer energetics and human obesity. *PLoS One.* 7(7): e40503.
- The Hazda are modern-day hunter-gatherers who have an average BMI of 20 vs. 27 for Western people
- But the average daily energy expenditure from physical activity is the same for the Hazda and Western people after controlling for body size
- Therefore, the difference in BMI is likely due to the hunter-gatherer diet vs. the Western diet

Rudman D et al. (1973). Maximal rates of excretion and synthesis of urea in normal and cirrhotic subjects. *J Clin Invest.* 52(9): 2241–2249.
- Human protein limit is 200-300 grams per day

Osterdahl M et al. (2008). Effects of a short-term intervention with a paleolithic diet in healthy volunteers. *Eur J Clin Nutr.* 62(5): 682–685.
- 20 medical students (average BMI: 22.2; average blood pressure: 110/65) were placed on a Paleo diet (fruits, vegetables, lean protein, fish) for 3 weeks
- Average BMI decreased to 21.4 and blood pressure decreased to 104/61

Aune D et al. (2016). BMI and all cause mortality: systematic review and non-linear dose-response meta-analysis of 230 cohort studies with 3.74 million deaths among 30.3 million participants. *BMJ.* 353: i2156.
- BMI of 20-22 is associated with lowest all-cause mortality

Whitlock G et al. (2009). Body-mass index and cause-specific mortality in 900 000 adults: collaborative analyses of 57 prospective studies. *Lancet.* 373(9669): 1083–1096.
- BMI of 30-35 is associated with 2-4 years of reduced longevity
- BMI of 40-45 is associated with 8-10 years of reduced longevity

Red meat

Daley CA et al. (2010). A review of fatty acid profiles and antioxidant content in grass-fed and grain-fed beef. *Nutr J.* 9: 10.
- The average omega-6 to omega-3 ratio in grass-fed beef is 1.53 vs. 7.65 for grain-fed beef
- Beta-carotene levels are 7 times higher in grass-fed vs. grain-fed beef

Pan A et al. (2011). Red meat consumption and risk of type 2 diabetes: 3 cohorts of US adults and an updated meta-analysis. *Am J Clin Nutr.* 94(4): 1088–1096.
- Red meat, and especially processed red meat, increases risk of Type 2 diabetes

Wang X et al. (2015). Red and processed meat consumption and mortality: dose-response meta-analysis of prospective cohort studies. *Public Health Nutr.* 19(5):893-905.
- Higher consumption of total red meat and processed meat is associated with an increased risk of total, cardiovascular and cancer mortality

Pan A et al. (2012). Red meat consumption and mortality: results from 2 prospective cohort studies. *Arch Intern Med.* 172(7): 555–563.
- Substituting 1 serving/day of red meat with fish/chicken/nuts/legumes/low-fat dairy/whole grains is associated with 7-19% lower mortality risk

Bernstein AM et al. (2010). Major dietary protein sources and risk of coronary heart disease in women. *Circulation.* 122(9): 876–883.
- Eating red meat, non-processed red meat, and high-fat dairy is associated with higher risk of heart disease
- Eating chicken, fish, and nuts was associated with lower risk

Fish

Raji CA et al. (2014). Regular fish consumption and age-related brain gray matter loss. *Am J Prev Med.* 47(4): 444–451.
- Eating fish protects against age-related loss of brain gray matter

Kris-Etherton PM et al. (2002). Fish consumption, fish oil, omega-3 fatty acids, and cardiovascular disease. *Circulation.* 106(21): 2747–2757.
- Eating fish twice a week lowers risk for heart disease because of omega-3 fats

Mozaffarian D, Rimm EB. (2006). Fish intake, contaminants, and human health: evaluating the risks and the benefits. *JAMA.* 296(15): 1885–1899.
- Eating fish high in omega-3 once or twice a week reduces risk of coronary death by 36% and total mortality by 17%

Foran JA et al. (2005). Quantitative analysis of the benefits and risks of consuming farmed and wild salmon. *J Nutr.* 135(11): 2639–2643.
- Wild salmon has an omega 3/omega 6 ratio of about 10 vs. 4 for farmed salmon i.e., 2.5X more omega-3 in wild salmon

Pauletto P et al. (1996). Blood pressure and atherogenic lipoprotein profiles of fish-diet and vegetarian villagers in Tanzania: the Lugalawa study. *Lancet*. 348(9030): 784–788.
- A diet high in wild fish results in lower blood pressure and lower cholesterol than a vegetarian diet

Eggs

Blesso CN et al. (2013). Whole egg consumption improves lipoprotein profiles and insulin sensitivity to a greater extent than yolk-free egg substitute in individuals with metabolic syndrome. *Metabolism*. 62(3): 400–410.
- Eating three whole eggs per day improves lipoprotein profiles and insulin sensitivity more than yolk-free egg substitutes

Valentine N et al. (2010). Daily egg consumption in hyperlipidemic adults - Effects on endothelial function and cardiovascular risk. *Nutr J*. 9:28.
- Eating eggs every day for six weeks improved endothelial function and lowered total cholesterol

Nuts

Aune D et al. (2016). Nut consumption and risk of cardiovascular disease, total cancer, all-cause and cause-specific mortality: a systematic review and dose-response meta-analysis of prospective studies. *BMC Med*. 14(1): 207.
- A meta-analysis of 20 studies found that eating nuts is associated with a lower risk of cardiovascular disease, cancer, death, respiratory disease, diabetes, and infections

Luu HN et al. (2015). Prospective evaluation of the association of nut/peanut consumption with total and cause-specific mortality. *JAMA Intern Med*. 175(5): 755–766.
- Eating nuts is associated with lower risk of death, and cardiovascular death

Fats

de Souza RJ et al. (2015). Intake of saturated and trans unsaturated fatty acids and risk of all cause mortality, cardiovascular disease, and type 2 diabetes: systematic review and meta-analysis of observational studies. *BMJ*. 351: h3978.
- Saturated fats are not associated with all-cause mortality, heart disease, stroke, or Type 2 diabetes

Pimpin L et al. (2016). Is butter back? A systematic review and meta-analysis of butter consumption and risk of cardiovascular disease, diabetes, and total mortality. *PLoS One*. 11(6): e0158118.
- Butter consumption has a very small or neutral association with mortality, heart disease, and diabetes

Mozaffarian D et al. (2006). Trans fatty acids and cardiovascular disease. *N Engl J Med*. 354(15): 1601–1613.
- Trans fats increase heart disease

Fruits and vegetables

Muraki I et al. (2013). Fruit consumption and risk of type 2 diabetes: results from three prospective longitudinal cohort studies. *BMJ*. 347: f5001.
- Eating whole fruits is associated with lower risk of Type 2 diabetes
- Consuming fruit juice is associated with higher risk

Wang X et al. (2014). Fruit and vegetable consumption and mortality from all causes, cardiovascular disease, and cancer: systematic review and dose-response meta-analysis of prospective cohort studies. *BMJ*. 349: g4490.
- Eating fruits and vegetables is associated with lower risk of death, especially cardiovascular death

Oyebode O et al. (2014). Fruit and vegetable consumption and all-cause, cancer and CVD mortality: analysis of Health Survey for England data. *J Epidemiol Community Health*. 68(9): 856–862.
- Eating fruits and vegetables is associated with lower risks of death, cancer, and heart disease
- Song M et al. (2016). Association of animal and plant protein intake With all-cause and cause-specific mortality. JAMA Intern Med. 176(10): 1453–1463.
- Eating more plant protein instead of red processed meat reduces total mortality and cardiovascular mortality

Smarter

Valls-Pedret C et al. (2015). Mediterranean diet and age-related cognitive decline: A randomized clinical trial. *JAMA Intern Med*. 175(7): 1094–1103.
- People eating a Mediterranean diet (fruit, vegetables, fish, chicken, legumes, olive oil, nuts, eggs) had improved memory, attention, and other cognitive function over 6 years

Happier

Mujcic R, Oswald A. (2016). Evolution of well-being and happiness after increases in consumption of fruit and vegetables. *Am J Public Health*. 106(8): 1504–1510.
- Increased fruit and vegetable consumption was predictive of increased happiness, life satisfaction, and well-being
- The increases were up to 0.24 life-satisfaction points for 8 portions a day, which is equal in size to the psychological gain of moving from unemployment to employment
- Improvements occurred within 24 months

Breymeyer KL et al. (2016). Subjective mood and energy levels of healthy weight and overweight/obese healthy adults on high-and low-glycemic load experimental diets. *Appetite.* 107:253-259.
- High-glycemic vs. low-glycemic diet resulted in 38% improved score for depressive symptoms, 55% improved score for total mood disturbance, and 26% improved score for fatigue/inertia

Junk food, juice, sugar

O'Connor L et al. (2015). Prospective associations and population impact of sweet beverage intake and type 2 diabetes, and effects of substitutions with alternative beverages. *Diabetologia.* 58(7): 1474-1483.
- Drinking sweetened beverages or sweetened tea/coffee increases risk of diabetes

McKeown NM et al. (2004). Carbohydrate nutrition, insulin resistance, and the prevalence of the metabolic syndrome in the Framingham Offspring Cohort. *Diabetes Care.* 27(2): 538-546.
- Eating high-glycemic food is associated with insulin resistance and metabolic syndrome
- Eating fiber reduces insulin resistance and metabolic syndrome

Ren YF, Amin A, Malmstrom H. (2009). Effects of tooth whitening and orange juice on surface properties of dental enamel. *J Dent.* 37(6): 424-431.
- Orange juice erodes dental enamel

Yang Q et al. (2014). Added sugar intake and cardiovascular diseases mortality among US adults. *JAMA Intern Med.* 174(4): 516-524.
- Eating sugar increases risk for cardiovascular death

Boden G et al. (2015). Excessive caloric intake acutely causes oxidative stress, GLUT4 carbonylation, and insulin resistance in healthy men. *Sci Transl Med.* 7(304): 304re7.
- Participants ate 6,000 kcal/day of the common US diet (50% carbohydrates, 35% fat, 15% protein) for 1 week
- There was a rapid weight gain of 3.5 kg and onset of insulin resistance

Breakfast

Blom WA et al. (2006). Effect of a high-protein breakfast on the postprandial ghrelin response. *Am J Clin Nutr.* 83(2): 211-220.
- High-protein breakfast decreases later hunger compared to high-carbohydrate breakfast

Reis CE et al. 2013). Acute and second-meal effects of peanuts on glycaemic response and appetite in obese women with high type 2 diabetes risk: a randomised crossover clinical trial. *Br J Nutr.* 109(11): 2015-2023.
- Peanut butter for breakfast reduces glycemic response and controls hunger

Mahoney CR et al. (2005). Effect of breakfast composition on cognitive processes in elementary school children. *Physiol Behav.* 85(5): 635–645.
- Eating oatmeal instead of high-glycemic breakfast results in better cognitive performance

Benton D, Parker PY. (1998). Breakfast, blood glucose, and cognition. *Am J Clin Nutr.* 67(4): 772S–778S.
- Eating breakfast improves memory and recall

Ingwersen J et al. (2007). A low glycaemic index breakfast cereal preferentially prevents children's cognitive performance from declining throughout the morning. *Appetite.* 49(1): 240–244.
- Low-glycemic index breakfast prevents declines in attention and memory throughout the morning

5. SCHEDULE 1 HOUR OF UNINTERRUPTED TIME FOR YOUR MOST IMPORTANT PROJECT

Szpunar KK, Moulton ST, Schacter DL. (2013). Mind wandering and education: from the classroom to online learning. *Front Psychol.* 4: 495.
- Most attention spans range from 18-40 minutes

Lee KE et al. (2015). 40-second green roof views sustain attention: The role of micro-breaks in attention restoration. *Journal of Environmental Psychology.* 42: 182–189.
- Taking a micro break of 40 seconds and looking at a flowering meadow green roof was better at restoring attention

Park AE et al. (2017). Intraoperative "micro breaks" with targeted stretching enhance surgeon physical function and mental focus: A multicenter cohort study. *Ann Surg.* 265: 340–346.
- Surgeons had less muscle pain and experienced better physical performance and mental focus when they took 1.5-2 minute stretching breaks at 20-40 minute intervals throughout their surgery cases

Chellappa SL, Gordijn MC, Cajochen C. (2011). Can light make us bright? Effects of light on cognition and sleep. *Prog Brain Res.* 190: 119–133.
- Bright light in the workplace improves cognitive performance, especially attention

Rubinstein JS, Meyer DE, Evans JE. (2001). Executive control of cognitive processes in task switching. *J Exp Psychol Hum Percept Perform.* 27(4): 763–797.
- Switching tasks resulted in slower performance than doing one task at a time

Leroy S. (2009). Why is it so hard to do my work? The challenge of attention residue when switching between work tasks. *Organizational Behavior and Human Decision Processes.* 109: 168–181.
- It is difficult for people to transition their attention away from an unfinished

task and this causes their performance to suffer on the new task

Furnham A, Bradley A. (1997). Music while you work: The differential distraction of background music on the cognitive test performance of introverts and extraverts. *Applied Cognitive Psychology*. 11: 445–455.
- Background music decreased performance on memory and comprehension tests, especially for introverts compared to extraverts

Knez I, Hygge S. (2002). Irrelevant speech and indoor lighting: Effects on cognitive performance and self-reported affect. *Applied Cognitive Psychology*. 16: 709–718.
- Background conversational speech impaired learning
- Warm white lighting improved memory recall

Perham N, Vizard J. (2010). Can preference for background music mediate the irrelevant sound effect? *Appl Cognit Psychol*. 25(4): 625–631.
- Cognitive performance was not impaired by listening to the same sound repeated, but was impaired by listening to different sounds and music

Mehta R, Zhu R, Cheema A. (2012). Is noise always bad? Exploring the effects of ambient noise on creative cognition. *Journal of Consumer Research*. 39(4): 784–799.
- A moderate level of ambient noise (70 decibels) improved performance on creative tasks
- A high level of ambient noise (85 decibels) impaired creativity

Kushlev K, Proulx J, Dunn EW. (2016). "Silence your phones": Smartphone notifications increase inattention and hyperactivity symptoms. *Proceedings of the 2016 CHI Conference on Human Factors in Computing Systems*. Pages 1011–1020.
- Interruptions from smartphone notification alerts resulted in poorer attention and hyperactivity, which in turn predicted lower productivity and poorer psychological well-being

Stothart C, Mitchum A, Yehnert C. (2015). The attentional cost of receiving a cell phone notification. *J Exp Psychol Hum Percept Perform*. 41(4): 893–897.
- Auditory or tactile cell phone notifications disrupted attention even if the participant did not interact with the phone
- The distraction effects were comparable to actually using the phone for voice calls or text messaging

6. TAKE TWO 10-MINUTE WALK BREAKS

Rhee H, Kim S. (2016). Effects of breaks on regaining vitality at work: An empirical comparison of 'conventional' and 'smart phone' breaks. *Computers in Human Behavior*. 57: 160–167.
- Taking restful breaks increased energy and reduced emotional exhaustion

Oppezzo M, Schwartz DL. (2014). Give your ideas some legs: the positive effect of walking on creative thinking. *J Exp Psychol Learn Mem Cogn.* 40(4): 1142–1152.
- Going for a walk improves creativity

Sonnentag S, Fritz C. 2015). Recovery from job stress: The stressor-detachment model as an integrative framework. *J Organiz Behav.* 36: S72–S103.
- Mentally disengaging from one's job while away from work is important for avoiding burnout and lower life satisfaction

Dababneh AJ, Swanson N, Shell RL. (2001). Impact of added rest breaks on the productivity and well being of workers. *Ergonomics.* 44(2): 164–174.
- 9-minute rest breaks for every 51 minutes of work decreased muscle discomfort for manual laborers

Boucsein W, Thum M. (1997). Design of work/rest schedules for computer work based on psychophysiological recovery measures. *International Journal of Industrial Ergonomics.* 20: 51–57.
- For computer workers, a 7.5 minute break after 50 minutes of work was most effective at reducing mental and emotional strain during the morning and early afternoon, whereas a 15 minute break after 100 minutes of work was more effective in the late afternoon

Througakos JP et al. (2008). Making the break count: An episodic examination of recovery activities, emotional experiences, and positive affective displays. *Academy of Management Journal.* 51(1): 131–146.
- Taking restful breaks increased positive emotions

Felsten G. (2009). Where to take a study break on the college campus: An attention restoration theory perspective. *Journal of Environmental Psychology.* 29: 160–167.
- Rest breaks involving exposure to nature were better at restoring attention

Kjellgren A, Buhrkall H. (2010). A comparison of the restorative effect of a natural environment with that of a simulated natural environment. *Journal of Environmental Psychology.* 30: 464–472.
- 30 minutes of relaxation in a natural environment was more restorative than an indoor simulation of the same environment

Berman MG, Jonides J, Kaplan S. (2008). The cognitive benefits of interacting with nature. *Psychol Sci.* 19(12): 1207–1212.
- Walking in nature or viewing pictures of nature improved performance on tasks requiring attention

7. READ FOR 30 MINUTES

Cunningham AE, Stanovich KE. (2001). What reading does for the mind. *Journal of Direct Instruction.* 1(2): 137–149.
- Reading increases vocabulary, general knowledge, spelling, and verbal fluency

Cunningham AE, Stanovich KE. (1993). Where does knowledge come from? Specific associations between print exposure and information acquisition. *Journal of Educational Psychology.* 85(2): 211–229.
- Reading increases general knowledge

Wilson RS et al. (2013). Life-span cognitive activity, neuropathologic burden, and cognitive aging. *Neurology.* 81(4): 314–321.
- Lifetime cognitive activity such as reading and writing was associated with slower cognitive decline during the last 6 years of life

Rayner K et al. (2016). So much to read, so little time: How do we read, and can speed reading help? *Psychol Sci Public Interest.* 17(1): 4–34.
- The way to read faster and maintain comprehension is to practice reading and expand your vocabulary
- Speed reading courses like Evelyn Wood increase speed at the expense of comprehension and accuracy

8. DO A GRATITUDE EXERCISE

Jackowska M et al. (2016). The impact of a brief gratitude intervention on subjective well-being, biology and sleep. *J Health Psychol.* 21(10): 2207–2217.
- Writing in a gratitude diary for 3 times/week for 2 weeks resulted in higher happiness, better sleep, and lower blood pressure

O'Leary K, Dockray S. (2015). The effects of two novel gratitude and mindfulness interventions on well-being. *J Altern Complement Med.* 21(4): 243–245.
- Writing in a gratitude diary for 4 times/week for 3 weeks resulted in more happiness and less stress

DeSteno D et al. (2014). Gratitude: a tool for reducing economic impatience. *Psychol Sci.* 25(6): 1262–1267.
- Gratitude increased patience for delaying gratification of financial rewards

Emmons RA, McCullough ME. (2003). Counting blessings versus burdens: an experimental investigation of gratitude and subjective well-being in daily life. *J Pers Soc Psychol.* 84(2): 377–389.
- Performing a gratitude exercise before bedtime every day for 2 weeks resulted in significantly more positive emotions (attentive, determined, energetic, enthusiastic, excited, interested, joyful, strong)

9. GET A GOOD NIGHT'S SLEEP

Healthier

Belenky G et al. (2003). Patterns of performance degradation and restoration during sleep restriction and subsequent recovery: a sleep dose-response study. *J Sleep Res.* 12(1): 1–12.

- Sleep deprivation reduces reaction time

Walker MP et al. (2002). Practice with sleep makes perfect: sleep-dependent motor skill learning. *Neuron.* 35(1): 205–211.
- A night of sleep resulted in a 20% increase in motor speed performance without loss of accuracy compared to the same period of time spent awake

Taffinder NJ et al. (1998). Effect of sleep deprivation on surgeons' dexterity on laparoscopy simulator. *Lancet.* 352(9135): 1191.
- Surgeons who had been awake all night made 20% more errors with a laparoscopic simulator and took 14% longer to complete the tasks than surgeons who had a full night of sleep

Ayas NT et al. (2006). Extended work duration and the risk of self-reported percutaneous injuries in interns. *JAMA.* 296(9): 1055–1062.
- Sleep deprivation increases risk of needlestick injuries in medical interns

Bryant PA, Trinder J, Curtis N. (2004). Sick and tired: Does sleep have a vital role in the immune system? *Nat Rev Immunol.* 4(6): 457–467.
- Sleep deprivation impairs the immune system

Cohen S et al. (2009). Sleep habits and susceptibility to the common cold. *Arch Intern Med.* 169(1): 62–67.
- Participants who averaged less than 7 hours of sleep over the past 14 days were 2.94 times more likely to develop a cold after being deliberately infected with rhinovirus compared with those who averaged >8 hours of sleep

Lange T et al. (2003). Sleep enhances the human antibody response to hepatitis A vaccination. *Psychosom Med.* 65(5): 831–835.
- Participants were injected with Hepatitis A vaccine and one group had a regular night's sleep and the other group didn't sleep for 24 hours
- 4 weeks later, the group who slept had generated nearly twice the number of Hep A antibodies

Leproult R, Van Cauter E. (2010). Role of sleep and sleep loss in hormonal release and metabolism. *Endocr Dev.* 17: 11–21.
- Sleep deprivation results in decreased glucose tolerance, decreased insulin sensitivity, higher evening concentrations of cortisol, higher levels of ghrelin ("hunger hormone"), decreased levels of leptin ("satiety hormone"), and increased hunger and appetite

Spiegel K, Leproult R, Van Cauter E. (1999). Impact of sleep debt on metabolic and endocrine function. *Lancet.* 354(9188): 1435–1439.
- Sleep restriction to 4 hours per night for 6 nights led to lower glucose tolerance and higher evening cortisol concentrations

Leproult R et al. (1997). Sleep loss results in an elevation of cortisol levels the next

evening. *Sleep.* 20(10): 865–870.
- Sleeping for 4 hours at night instead of 8 hours led to a 37% increase in the levels of stress-hormone cortisol the next day

de Mello MT et al. (2013). Sleep disorders as a cause of motor vehicle collisions. *Int J Prev Med.* 4(3): 246–257.
- Driver fatigue is linked to 16-20% of serious highway accidents

Smarter

Diekelmann S, Born J. (2010). The memory function of sleep. *Nat Rev Neurosci.* 11(2): 114–126.
- Sleep improves memory and learning

Van Dongen HP et al. (2003). The cumulative cost of additional wakefulness: dose-response effects on neurobehavioral functions and sleep physiology from chronic sleep restriction and total sleep deprivation. *Sleep.* 26(2): 117–126.
- Sleeping 6 hours instead of 8 hours a night led to cognitive performance deficits
- Participants were largely unaware of these deficits, which may explain why many people assume that getting less sleep has minimal side effects

Landrigan CP et al. (2004). Effect of reducing interns' work hours on serious medical errors in intensive care units. *N Engl J Med.* 351(18): 1838–1848.
- Medical interns made 35.9% more serious medical errors when they were on call for 24 hours or more every third night vs. not being on call

Wagner DT et al. (2012). Lost sleep and cyberloafing: Evidence from the laboratory and a daylight saving time quasi-experiment. *J Appl Psychol.* 97(5): 1068–1076.
- Sleep deprivation and low-quality sleep resulted in more cyberloafing
- The shift to Daylight Savings Time (DST) greatly increased cyberloafing on the following workday

Dawson D, Reid K. (1997). Fatigue, alcohol and performance impairment. *Nature.* 388(6639): 235.
- 24 hours of sustained wakefulness was equivalent to a blood alcohol concentration of 0.10% for cognitive psychomotor performance (the legal limit for driving is 0.08%)

Pilcher JJ et al. (2015). Interactions between sleep habits and self-control. *Front Hum Neurosci.* 9: 284.

Sleep deprivation impairs self-control

Stickgold R, James L, Hobson JA. (2000). Visual discrimination learning requires sleep after training. *Nat Neurosci.* 3(12): 1237–1238.
- Sleeping within 30 hours of training is required for improved performance

Wagner U et al. (2004). Sleep inspires insight. *Nature.* 427(6972): 352–355.

- Participants were trained on a puzzle with a hidden shortcut
- Those who got 8 hours of sleep after the training were more than twice as likely to see the shortcut than those who stayed awake for 8 hours (59.1% vs. 22.7%)

Better social skills

Simon EB et al. (2015). Losing neutrality: The neural basis of impaired emotional control without sleep. *J Neurosci.* 35(38): 13194–13205.
- Sleep deprivation impairs emotional control

Goldstein-Piekarski AN et al. (2015). Sleep deprivation impairs the human central and peripheral nervous system discrimination of social threat. *J Neurosci.* 35(28): 10135–10145.
- Sleep deprivation impairs assessment of facial expressions

Happier

Peach H et al. (2016). Sleep hygiene and sleep quality as predictors of positive and negative dimensions of mental health in college students. *Cogent Psych.* 3: 1168768.
- Worse sleep quality was associated with more depressive symptoms and lower subjective well-being

Dinges DF et al. (1997). Cumulative sleepiness, mood disturbance, and psychomotor vigilance performance decrements during a week of sleep restricted to 4-5 hours per night. *Sleep.* 20(4): 267-277.
- Sleep restriction of 5 hours a night for 7 consecutive nights led to higher confusion, tension, poorer mood, mental exhaustion, and stress

Zohar D et al. (2005). The effects of sleep loss on medical residents' emotional reactions to work events: a cognitive-energy model. *Sleep.* 28(1): 47–54.
- Sleep disruption in medical residents led to more negative emotions and less positive emotions

Hamilton NA et al. (2007). Sleep and psychological well-being. *Soc Indic Res.* 82(1): 147–163.
- People who slept between 6-8.5 hours per night reported fewer symptoms of depression, and anxiety, and reported higher levels of environmental mastery, personal growth, positive relations with others, purpose in life, and self-acceptance

How to get a better night's sleep

Hirshkowitz M et al. (2015). National Sleep Foundation's sleep time duration recommendations: methodology and results summary. *Sleep Health.* 1: 40–43.
- The National Sleep Foundation recommends that adults aged 18-64 get 7-9 hours of sleep a night

Yetish G et al. (2015). Natural sleep and its seasonal variations in three pre-industrial societies. *Curr Biol.* 25(21): 2862–2868.
- People living in preindustrial societies in Tanzania, Namibia, and Bolivia sleep an average of 6.9-8.5 hours (5.7-7.1 hours of actual sleep time)
- Sleep onset is about 3.3 hours after sunset
- Sleep occurs during the nightly period of falling temperature
- There is little napping
- Light exposure is maximal in the morning

Potter GDM et al. (2016). Circadian rhythm and sleep disruption: Causes, metabolic consequences and countermeasures. *Endocr Rev.* 37(6): 584–608.
- People have a circadian rhythm with a period of about 24 hours
- The term "social jetlag" refers to different bed times on work days and non-work days and it is associated with obesity and insulin resistance

Wong PM et al. (2015). Social jetlag, chronotype, and cardiometabolic risk. *J Clin Endocrinol Metab.* 100(12): 4612–4620.
- Social jetlag was related to higher triglycerides, insulin resistance, and obesity

Zhdanova IV et al. (1998). Endogenous melatonin levels and the fate of exogenous melatonin: Age effects. *J Gerontol A Biol Sci Med Sci.* 53(4): B293–298.
- Melatonin levels start rising around 9pm and drop to low levels around 7-9am

Brown GM. (1994). Light, melatonin and the sleep-wake cycle. *J Psychiatry Neurosci.* 19(5): 345–353.
- Blood levels of melatonin are high at night and low during the day
- Melatonin secretion is reduced by exposure to light
- Melatonin induces drowsiness and sleep

Magnusson A, Kristbjarnarson H. (1991). Treatment of seasonal affective disorder with high-intensity light. *J Affect Disord.* 21(2): 141–147.
- 40-minute exposure to 10,000 lux white light improved depression symptom in patients with seasonal affectivity disorder

Chang AM et al. (2015). Evening use of light-emitting eReaders negatively affects sleep, circadian timing, and next-morning alertness. *Proc Natl Acad Sci USA.* 112(4): 1232–1237.
- Participants reading a light-emitting device eBook in the hours before bedtime took longer to fall asleep, had reduced evening sleepiness, reduced melatonin secretion, later timing of their circadian clock, and reduced next-morning alertness

TIME MANAGEMENT

BENEFITS OF TIME MANAGEMENT

Foroughi CK et al. (2014). Do interruptions affect quality of work? *Hum Factors.* 56(7): 1262–1271.
- 54 students performed a creative writing task with and without interruptions
- Interruptions significantly worsened the quality and quantity of work

Amabile TM, Hadley CN, Kramer SJ. (2002). Creativity under the gun. *Harvard Business Review.* 80(8): 52–464.
- Time diaries from 177 employees found that on days with the most time pressure, people were 45% less likely to think creatively than on any of the lower-pressure days

Masicampo EJ, Baunmeister RF. (2011). Consider it done! Plan making can eliminate the cognitive effects of unfulfilled goals. *J Pers Soc Psychol.* 101(4): 667–683.
- Unfulfilled goals persist in the mind and lead to intrusive thoughts, but making a specific plan eliminates this effect and frees up mental resources

BENEFITS OF CONSCIENTIOUSNESS

Heckman JJ, Kautz T. (2012). Hard evidence on soft skills. *Labour Econ.* 19(4): 451–464.
- Conscientiousness is defined as "the tendency to be organized, responsible, and hardworking" and is related to grit, perseverance, delay of gratification, impulse control, achievement striving, ambition, and work ethic
- Conscientiousness increases with age

Jackson JJ et al. (2010). What do conscientious people do? Development and validation of the Behavioral Indicators of Conscientiousness (BIC). *J Res Pers.* 44(4): 501–511.
- Conscientious people are more likely to do the following behaviors: label drawers in my office, use a planner to schedule the days' events, cross off items from my to do list, make an itinerary, file papers in a desk drawer, make lists, use a calendar or date book to plan my activities, file financial documents, organize work files and materials in a systematic manner, use a file system for important papers, write in a date book, set a timeline for getting a project done, persist at tasks after meeting setbacks or failures, work extra hard on a project to make sure that it is done right, complete the projects I start, get to appointments on time, allow extra time for getting lost when going to new places, complete assignments on time, show up for work more than 5 min early, get to work on time, return phone calls and emails in a timely fashion, keep up with required work, fulfill an obligation to someone, double-check my work, proofread my writing, pay bills on time

Back MD, Schmukle S, Egloff B. (2006). Who is late and who is early? Big Five personality factors and punctuality in attending psychological experiments. *J Res Pers*. 40(5): 841–848.
- Conscientiousness is a significant predictor of punctuality

Bogg T, Roberts BW. (2013). The case for conscientiousness: Evidence and implications for a personality trait marker of health and longevity. *Ann Behav Med*. 45(3): 278–288.
- Conscientiousness is associated with longevity, lower risk of Alzheimer's disease, lower stress, healthy eating, and lower likelihood of risky behaviors such as alcohol abuse, drug use, risky sex, risky driving, tobacco use, suicide, and violence

Bartley CE, Roesch SC. (2011). Coping with daily stress: The role of conscientiousness. *Pers Individ Dif*. 50(1): 79–83.
- Conscientious people experience less daily stress

Duggan KA et al. (2014). Personality and healthy sleep: The importance of conscientiousness and neuroticism. *PLoS One*. 9(3): e90628.
- Conscientiousness is a significant predictor of good sleep

Hayes N, Joseph S. (2003). Big 5 correlates of three measures of subjective well-being. *Pers Individ Dif*. 34(4): 723–727.
- Conscientious people have higher life satisfaction

Noftle EE, Robins RW. (2007). Personality predictors of academic outcomes: Big Five correlates of GPA and SAT Scores. *J Pers Soc Psychol*. 93(1): 116–130.
- Conscientiousness is the strongest personality predictor of high school and college GPA scores

Schmidt FL, Hunter J. (2004). General mental ability in the world of work: Occupational attainment and job performance. *J Pers Soc Psychol*. 86(1): 162–173.
- Conscientiousness is a significant predictor of career success and job performance

Duckworth AL et al. (2012). Who does well in life? Conscientious adults excel in both objective and subjective success. *Front Psychol*. 3: 356.
- Conscientious adults earned more money over their lifetimes and ended up with more savings e.g., adults who were in the top 30% of conscientiousness earned an additional $96,000 over their lifetimes
- Conscientious adults experienced more positive and less negative emotion, and were more satisfied with their lives

TIME MANAGEMENT SYSTEM

Allen D. (2003). *Getting things done: The art of stress-free productivity*. Penguin Books.
- 4 Ds of getting things done: Delete, Delegate, Do, and Defer

Todd JJ, Marois R. (2004). Capacity limit of visual short-term memory in human posterior parietal cortex. *Nature.* 428(6984):751–754.
- Short-term memory has a capacity limit of 3-4 items

Stothart C, Mitchum A, Yehnert C. (2015). The attentional cost of receiving a cell phone notification. *J Exp Psychol Hum Percept Perform.* 41(4): 893–897.
- Auditory or tactile cell phone notifications disrupted attention even if the participant did not interact with the phone
- The distraction effects were comparable to actually using the phone for voice calls or text messaging

Rubinstein JS, Meyer DE, Evans JE. (2001). Executive control of cognitive processes in task switching. *J Exp Psychol Hum Percept Perform.* 27(4): 763–797.
- Switching tasks resulted in slower performance than doing one task at a time

Leroy S. (2009). Why is it so hard to do my work? The challenge of attention residue when switching between work tasks. *Organizational Behavior and Human Decision Processes.* 109: 168–181.
- It is difficult for people to transition their attention away from an unfinished task and this causes their performance to suffer on the new task

Perham N, Vizard J. (2010). Can preference for background music mediate the irrelevant sound effect? *Appl Cognit Psychol.* 25(4): 625–631.
- Cognitive performance was not impaired by listening to the same sound repeated, but was impaired by listening to different sounds and music

CREATIVE PROBLEM SOLVING

INTRODUCTION

Johannes Gutenberg. (n.d.). In *Wikipedia.* Retrieved July 23, 2020, from https://en.wikipedia.org/wiki/Johannes_Gutenberg

IDENTIFY THE RIGHT PROBLEM

Scott G, Leritz LE, Mumford MD. (2004). The effectiveness of creativity training: A quantitative review. *Creat Res J.* 16(4): 361–388.
- Effective creativity training includes processes for problem finding, conceptual combination, and idea generation

Gallate J et al. (2012). Creative people use nonconscious processes to their advantage. *Creat Res J.* 24(2-3): 146–151.
- The stages of creativity include preparation (a problem is isolated, organized, and targeted), incubation, insight, and verification (testing and applying the solution)
- More solutions are produced after a break than working continuously on a problem

PREPARE YOUR KNOWLEDGE

Heilman KM, Nadeau SE, Beversdorf DO. (2003). Creative innovation: Possible brain mechanisms. *Neurocase.* 9(5): 369-379.
- A high level of domain-specific knowledge, concepts, and special skills are important for creativity

Simonton DK. (2000). Creative development as acquired expertise: Theoretical issues and an empirical test. *Developmental Review.* 20(2): 283-318.
- Creativity is increased by complex specialization ("overtraining") and versatility ("cross-training")

Root-Bernstein R et al. (2008). Arts foster scientific success: Avocations of Nobel, National Academy, Royal Society, and Sigma Xi Members. *Journal of Psychology of Science and Technology.* 1(2): 51-63.
- Nobel laureates and top scientists were more likely to have arts and craft hobbies than regular scientists and the general public

GENERATE LOTS OF SOLUTIONS

Jung RE et al. (2015). Quantity yields quality when it comes to creativity: a brain and behavioral test of the equal-odds rule. *Front Psychol.* 6: 864.
- Higher number of responses on a divergent thinking task led to higher creativity

Carson SH, Peterson JB, Higgins DM. (2003). Decreased latent inhibition is associated with increased creative achievement in high-functioning individuals. *J Pers Soc Psychol.* 85(3): 499-506.
- Creative achievers were more likely to demonstrate less latent inhibition i.e., they were less likely to screen out irrelevant or unusual thoughts from their minds

Colombo B et al. (2015). The combined effects of neurostimulation and priming on creative thinking. A preliminary tDCS study on dorsolateral prefrontal cortex. *Front Hum Neurosci.* 9: 403.
- Divergent priming increases creativity i.e., visualizing yourself using an object in an unusual way

Benedek M, Konen T, Neubauer AC. (2012). Associative abilities underlying creativity. *Psychology of Aesthetics, Creativity, and the Arts.* 6(3): 273-281.
- Divergent thinking is important for creativity, and an important component is the ability to make new associations

Andreasen NC, Ramchandran K. (2012). Creativity in art and science: are there two cultures? *Dialogues Clin Neurosci.* 14(1): 49-54.
- Brain scans of highly creative artists and scientists showed that they experienced high emotions and vivid imagery even during simple word association tasks

Chavez RA. (2016). Imagery as a core process in the creativity of successful and awarded artists and scientists and its neurobiological correlates. *Front Psychol.* 7: 351.
- Highly creative, internationally awarded scientists and artists showed high activation of their brain's imagery regions during creativity tasks

INCUBATE THE PROBLEM TO DISCOVER BETTER SOLUTIONS

Atchley RA, Strayer DL, Atchley P. (2012). Creativity in the wild: Improving creative reasoning through immersion in natural settings. *PLoS One.* 7(12): e51474.
- Four days of hiking in nature improved performance by 50% on a creative problem-solving task

Ritter SM, Dijksterhuis A. (2014). Creativity—the unconscious foundations of the incubation period. *Front Hum Neurosci.* 8: 215.
- When stuck on a creative task, you should do something undemanding that is very different from the task before returning to it
- Unconscious incubation works best if you've already established a large knowledge base and know what problems to tackle

Dijksterhuis A, Meurs T. (2006). Where creativity resides: The generative power of unconscious thought. *Conscious Cogn.* 15(1):135–146.
- Unconscious thought leads to more creativity and this may be because it is more divergent and associative than conscious thought

Baror S, Bar M. (2016). Associative activation and its relation to exploration and exploitation in the brain. *Psychol Sci.* 27(6): 776–789.
- Creativity is increased by keeping your mind clear of stray thoughts, obsessive ruminations, and other forms of "mental load"

Wagner U et al. (2004). Sleep inspires insight. *Nature.* 427(6972): 352–355.
- A night of sleep more than doubles the likelihood of discovering a novel solution to a math problem

Cai DJ et al. (2009). REM, not incubation, improves creativity by priming associative networks. *Proc Natl Acad Sci USA.* 106(25): 10130–10134.
- REM sleep improves creativity by priming associative networks in the brain

FINANCIAL FREEDOM

Adeney P. (2014). If you think this is about extreme frugality, you're missing the point. *Mr. Money Mustache.*

Adeney P. (2011). A brief history of the stash: How we saved from zero to retirement in 10 years. *Mr. Money Mustache.*

BENEFITS OF BEING RICH

Semyonov M, Lewin-Epstein N, Maskileyson D. (2013). Where wealth matters more for health: The wealth-health gradient in 16 countries. *Soc Sci Med*. 81: 10–17.
- In a study of 16 countries, rich people tended to be healthier than poor people

Chetty R et al. (2016). The association between income and life expectancy in the United States, 2001-2014. *JAMA*. 315(16): 1750–1766.
- In the United States, the gap in life expectancy between the richest 1% and the poorest 1% of people was 14.6 years

Parker K. (2012). Yes, the rich are different. *Pew Research Social & Demographic Trends*.
- 29% of those in the upper class say they frequently experience stress, compared with 37% of those in the middle class and 58% of lower-class adults

Stevenson B, Wolfers J. (2013). Subjective well-being and income: Is there any evidence of satiation? *CAMA Working Paper* 21/2013.
- Higher income is associated with higher subjective well-being

Kahneman D, Deaton A. (2010). High income improves evaluation of life but not emotional well-being. *Proc Natl Acad Sci USA*. 107(38): 16489–16493.
- Frequency and intensity of positive emotions such as joy and affection rise with income, but plateau at an annual income of about $75,000
- Low income is associated with low life evaluation and low emotional well-being

Ruberton PM, Gladstone J, Lyubomirsky S. (2016). How your bank balance buys happiness: The importance of "cash on hand" to life satisfaction. *Emotion*. 16(5): 575–580.
- Going from having £1 to £1,000 in one's bank account each month was associated with a 10% gain in life satisfaction from feeling more secure about one's finances Emotion
- Going from £1,000 to £10,000 was associated with a 3.5% gain in life satisfaction

RISKS OF BEING RICH

Piff PK et al. (2012). Higher social class predicts increased unethical behavior. *Proc Natl Acad Sci USA*. 109(11): 4086–4091.
- Rich people are more likely to lie, cheat, and do unethical things

Piff PK et al. (2010). Having less, giving more: The influence of social class on prosocial behavior. *J Pers Soc Psychol*. 99(5): 771–784.
- Rich people are less charitable and less compassionate

Dietze P, Knowles ED. (2016). Social class and the motivational relevance of other human beings: Evidence from visual attention. *Psychol Sci*. 27(11): 1517–1527.
- High-class people pay less attention to others

Quoidbach J et al. (2010). Money giveth, money taketh away: The dual effect of wealth on happiness. *Psychol Sci.* 21(6): 759–763.
- Access to the best things in life undercuts enjoyment from life's small pleasures

Luthar SS, Latendresse SJ. (2005). Children of the affluent: Challenges to well-being. *Curr Dir Psychol Sci.* 14(1): 49–53.
- Rich people's children have higher risks of drug use, anxiety, and depression caused by pressures to achieve and lack of quality time with their busy parents

PART TWO: INVEST YOUR SAVINGS

1. Invest in Vanguard's S&P 500 Index fund

Hamm T. (2013). What Warren Buffett's stock market math means for your retirement. *Christian Science Monitor.* May 6.
- Warren Buffett: "The economy, as measured by gross domestic product, can be expected to grow at an annual rate of about 3 percent over the long term, and inflation of 2 percent would push nominal GDP growth to 5 percent. Stocks will probably rise at about that rate and dividend payments will boost total returns to 6 percent to 7 percent."

Soe AM, Poirier R. (2016). SPIVA® U.S. mid-year 2016 scorecard. *S&P Dow Jones Indices.*
- "Over the 10-year investment horizon, 85.36% of large-cap managers, 91.27% of mid-cap managers, and 90.75% of small-cap managers failed to outperform [the index] on a relative basis"

Philips CB et al. (2014). The case for index-fund investing. *Vanguard.* April.
- Page 13, Figure 10: Actively-managed funds have Management Expense Ratios (MERs) of about 1.0% vs. 0.05% for Vanguard i.e., a 20X difference

PART THREE: EARN MORE MONEY WITH A SIDE BUSINESS

1. Start a business that brings an existing technology/product/service to a new market of users

Raffiee J, Feng J. (2014). Should I quit my day job?: A hybrid path to entrepreneurship. *Academy of Management Journal.* 57(4): 936-963.

LOVE YOUR WORK

Askinosie S, Askinosie L. (2017). *Meaningful work: a quest to do great business, find your calling, and feed your soul.*

Askinosie Chocolate. (2019). *Our story.*

Lyubomirsky S, King L, Diener E. (2005). The benefits of frequent positive affect: does happiness lead to success? *Psychol Bull.* 131(6): 803-855.
- Benefits of happiness include higher income, more good friends and social support, more fulfilling marriages, and better health

Ryan RM, Deci EL. (2001). On happiness and human potentials: a review of research on hedonic and eudaimonic well-being. *Annu Rev Psychol.* 52: 141–166.
- Achieving self-concordant goals leads to greater subjective well-being and psychological well-being

Sheldon KM, Elliot AJ. (1999). Goal striving, need satisfaction, and longitudinal well-being: the self-concordance model. *J Pers Soc Psychol.* 76(3): 482–497.
- Self-concordant goals are in accordance with our true selves, or our underlying feelings, values, and desires
- People invest greater long-term effort in achieving self-concordant goals and this increases the likelihood of success
- Achieving self-concordant goals leads to greater feelings of autonomy, competence, and relatedness

Deci EL, Ryan RM. (2000). The "what" and "why" of goal pursuits: Human needs and the self-determination of behavior. *Psychological Inquiry.* 11(4): 227–268.
- To be happy, your work must fulfill three universal psychological needs: autonomy (control over your work and time), competence (mastering useful things), and relatedness (to love and care, and to be loved and cared for)

Ericsson KA, Krampe RT. Tesh-Romer C. (1993). The role of deliberate practice in the acquisition of expert performance. *Psychological Review.* 100(3): 363–406.
- It takes a minimum of 10 years of deliberate practice to achieve expert performance

Wrzesniewski A et al. (1997). Jobs, careers, and callings: People's relations to their work. *J Res Pers.* 31(1): 21–33.
- Most people see their work as either a job (focus on financial rewards and necessity rather than pleasure or fulfillment; not a major positive part of life), a career (focus on advancement), or a calling (focus on enjoyment of fulfilling, socially useful work)
- About a third of people each see their work as a job, career, or calling
- Even in a lower-status occupation like administrative assistant, about a third each saw their work as a job, career, or calling

Sheldon KM. (2014). Becoming oneself: the central role of self-concordant goal selection. *Pers Soc Psychol Rev.* 18(4): 349–365.
- It can be difficult to find self-concordant goals because your brain uses two systems for thinking that operate largely independently from each other: "System 1" is non-conscious, parallel, intuitive/automatic, and evolutionarily older, and "System 2" is conscious, sequential, deliberate/controlled, and evolutionarily more recent

Burton CM. (2008). Gut feelings and goal pursuit: A path to selfconcordance. *Dissertation Abstracts International: Section B. Sciences and Engineering.* 73(2-B): 1303–1387.
- Listening to your gut can help find goals that are fulfilling

Brown KW, Ryan RM. (2003). The benefits of being present: mindfulness and its role in psychological well-being. *J Pers Soc Psychol.* 84(4): 822-848.
- Self-awareness can help you choose behaviors that are in accordance with your needs, values, and interests

Vago DR, Silbersweig DA. (2012). Self-awareness, self-regulation, and self-transcendence (S-ART): a framework for understanding the neurobiological mechanisms of mindfulness. *Front Hum Neurosci.* 6: 296.
- Meditation increases self-awareness

Job V, Brandstatter V. (2009). Get a taste of your goals: promoting motive-goal congruence through affect-focus goal fantasy. *J Pers.* 77(5): 1527–1559.
- To discover self-concordant goals, visualize achieving the goal and observe the emotions you feel

Boyatzis R, McKee A, Goleman D. (2002). Reawakening your passion for work. *Harv Bus Rev.* 80(4): 86–94.
- Stay in touch with what's important to you by scheduling "reflective structures", time and space for self-examination, whether a few hours a week, a day or two a month, or a longer period every year

Lekes N et al. (2012). Influencing value priorities and increasing well-being: The effects of reflecting on intrinsic values. *Journal of Positive Psychology.* 7(3): 249–261.
- Experience higher well-being by writing down the values that are important to you and reflecting on them weekly

Waterman AS et al. (2010). The Questionnaire for Eudaimonic Well-Being: Psychometric properties, demographic comparisons, and evidence of validity. *Journal of Positive Psychology.* 5(1): 41–61.
- Eudaimonic Well-Being (EWB) refers to quality of life derived from the development of a person's best potentials and applying them towards personally expressive, self-concordant goals
- The Questionnaire for Eudaimonic Well-Being (QEWB) was developed to measure well-being

Enron. (1999). *Enron Named One of '100 Best Companies to Work For in America'* [Press Release]. Retrieved from http://www.prnewswire.com/news-releases/enron-named-one-of-100-best-companies-to-work-for-in-america-77738922.html

WORK WORTH DOING
Scientific evidence

INTRODUCTION

Kubania J. (2015, July 6). How second-hand clothing donations are creating a dilemma for Kenya. *Guardian*.

Christensen CM, Ojomo E, Dillon K. (2019). *The prosperity paradox: How innovation can lift nations out of poverty*. Harper Collins.

1. SOLVE THE ROOT PROBLEM, NOT SYMPTOMS

Moyo D. (2009, March 21). Why foreign aid is hurting Africa. *Wall St J*.
- "Money from rich countries has trapped many African nations in a cycle of corruption, slower economic growth and poverty."

Munk N. (2016). How Warren Buffett's son would feed the world. *The Atlantic*. May.
- "Over the past decade, patiently, the Howard G. Buffett Foundation has spent hundreds of millions of dollars to identify and promote practical, low-cost methods of conservation farming—cover crops, no-till farming, locally bred seed varieties—that improve African soil quality and crop yields without chemical fertilizers and costly imported seeds."

2. LISTEN TO SMART PEOPLE WHO DISAGREE WITH YOU

Lord CG, Ross L, Lepper MR. (1979). Biased assimilation and attitude polarization: The effects of prior theories on subsequently considered evidence. *J Pers Soc Psychol*. 37(11): 2098-2109.
- "People who hold strong opinions on complex social issues are likely to examine evidence in a biased manner. They are apt to accept 'confirming' evidence at face value while subjecting 'disconfirming' evidence to critical evaluation, and as a result to draw undue support for their initial positions from mixed or random empirical findings."

Balcetis E, Dunning D. (2006). See what you want to see: motivational influences on visual perception. *J Pers Soc Psychol*. 91(4): 612-625.
- People's wishes and preferences influence the preconscious processing of visual stimuli in the brain so that you literally see what you want to see

Lilienfeld SO, Ammirati R, Landfield K. (2009). Giving debiasing away: Can psychological research on correcting cognitive errors promote human welfare? *Perspect Psychol Sci*. 4(4): 390-398.
- Two methods of debiasing people are:
  - "active open-mindedness" where you thoughtfully consider arguments on multiple sides of an issue
  - "consider-the-opposite" or "consider-an-alternative" strategies

Example: Increasing minimum wage

Luca DL, Luca M. (2017). Survival of the fittest: The impact of the minimum wage on firm exit. *Harvard Business School*. Working Paper 17-088.
- Each $1 increase in minimum wage leads to 4-10% increase in likelihood on firm exits in the restaurant industry

Macpherson D. (2017). The impact of an $11 minimum wage in St. Louis. *Employment Policies Institute*.
- "An $11 minimum wage in St. Louis would cost the city roughly 1,000 jobs, with the job loss mostly occurring among the city's most vulnerable populations."

Murphy RP, Lammam C, MacIntyre H. (2016). Raising the minimum wage: Misguided policy, unintended consequences. *Fraser Institute*.
- "Canadian empirical evidence suggests that a 10% increase in the minimum wage would lead to a 3% to 6% drop in youth employment"
- Raising minimum wage decreases employment opportunities among low-skilled workers who these policies were originally designed to help

WINNING STRATEGY

INTRODUCTION

Romance of the three kingdoms. (n.d.). In *Wikipedia*. Retrieved July 23, 2020, from https://en.wikipedia.org/wiki/Romance_of_the_Three_Kingdoms"

"Wikipedia. (2019). Zhuge Liang." to "Zhuge Liang. (n.d.). In *Wikipedia*. Retrieved July 23, 2020, from https://en.wikipedia.org/wiki/Zhuge_Liang"

NEW-MARKET DISRUPTIVE INNOVATIONS

Washburn AN, Skitka LJ. (2017). Science denial across the political divide: Liberals and conservatives are similarly motivated to deny attitude-inconsistent science. *Soc Psychol Personal Sci*. 9(8): 194855061773150.
- Both liberals and conservatives reject scientific facts that contradict their existing beliefs

Balcetis E, Dunning D. (2006). See what you want to see: motivational influences on visual perception. *J Pers Soc Psychol*. 91(4): 612–625.
- People's wishes and preferences influence the brain's preconscious processing of visual stimuli and this affects what is seen by conscious awareness

Reifler J, Nyhan B. (2010). When corrections fail: The persistence of political misperceptions. *Political Behavior*. 32(2): 303–330.
- Fact-checking that contradicts existing beliefs often entrenches those beliefs rather than changing them

Berns GS et al. (2005). Neurobiological correlates of social conformity and independence during mental rotation. *Biol Psychiatry.* 58(3): 245-253.
- People often change their minds to conform with a group because the social influence changes the way their brains perceive the information

Cialdini RB, Goldstein NJ. (2004). Social influence: compliance and conformity. *Annu Rev Psychol.* 55: 591-621.
- People change their minds to gain social approval and to fit in with the majority

McMillan J, Hanley D. (2003). Grameen Bank. *Stanford Graduate School of Business.* Case No. SM116.
- Case study and business model analysis

Gates Foundation. (1999, November 23). *Bill & Melinda Gates Foundation announces $750 million gift to speed delivery of life-saving vaccines* [Press Release].

LOW-END DISRUPTIVE INNOVATIONS

Christensen CM et al. (2006). Disruptive innovation for social change. *Harv Bus Rev.* 84(12): 94-101.

Beard A. (2014). Life's work: Salman Khan. *Harvard Business Review, The Magazine.* January-February.

Rangan VK, Thulasiraj RD. (2007). Making sight affordable (Innovations Case Narrative: The Aravind Eye Care System). *Innovations: Technology, Governance, Globalization.* 2(4): 35-49.
- Case study and business model analysis

WIN WITH PSYCHOLOGY

Starmans C, Sheskin M, Bloom P. (2017). Why people prefer unequal societies. *Nature Human Behavior.* 1(4): 0082..
- Humans have a deep-rooted preference for fairness

van 't Wout M et al. (2006). Affective state and decision-making in the Ultimatum Game. *Exp Brain Res.* 169(4): 564-568.
- People have strong emotional reactions to unfairness

Kaufman MR et al. (2016). Protect your loved ones from Fataki": Discouraging cross-generational sex in Tanzania. *Qual Health Res.* 26(7): 994-1004.
- The Fataki media campaign discouraged young women from having sex with older men

Engler M, Engler P. (2014). How did Gandhi win? *Waging Nonviolence.* October 8.

Mauss IB, Robinson MD. (2009). Measures of emotion: A review. *Cogn Emot.* 23(2): 209-237.
- Anger and fear are strong emotions

WIN BY FIGHTING INDIRECTLY

Arreguin-Toft I. (2001). How the weak win wars: a theory of asymmetric conflict. *International Security.* 26(1): 93-128.
- From 1800 to 1998, there were 170 wars around the world where the weaker side won 63 percent of the time when they fought indirectly

Vulliamy E. (1999, December 19). How drug giants let millions die of Aids. *Guardian.*

Swarns RL. (2001, April 20). Drug makers drop South Africa suit over AIDS medicine. *New York Times.*

Boseley S. (2016, January 26). Big Pharma's worst nightmare. *Guardian.*

POWER CORRUPTS

Anderson C, Galinsky AD. (2006). Power, optimism, and risk-taking. *Eur J Soc Psychol.* 36(4): 511-536.
- Feeling powerful increases optimism in perceiving risks and leads to more risky behavior
- These effects can be counteracted by feeling a sense of responsibility

Hogeveen J, Inzlicht M, Obhi SS. (2014). Power changes how the brain responds to others. *J Exp Psychol Gen.* 143(2): 755-762.
- Feeling powerful reduces the brain's empathy for others

Galinsky AD et al. (2006). Power and perspectives not taken. *Psychol Sci.* 17(12): 1068-1074.
- Feeling powerful reduces the ability to determine how other people see, think, and feel

Bernile G, Bhagwat V, Rau PR. (2017). What doesn't kill you will only make you more risk-loving: Early-life disasters and CEO behavior. *J Finance.* 72(1): 167-206.
- CEOs who experience early-life fatal disasters behave more conservatively and take less risk

ASSEMBLE A GREAT TEAM

BENEFITS OF WORKING WITH A TEAM

Laughlin PR et al. (2006). Groups perform better than the best individuals on letters-to-numbers problems: effects of group size. *J Pers Soc Psychol.* 90(4): 644-651.
- Groups solved a logic puzzle faster, more creatively, and with fewer errors than the best individual alone

Wuchty S, Jones BF, Uzzi B. (2007). The increasing dominance of teams in production of knowledge. *Science.* 316(5827): 1036-1039.
- Scientific teams produce better research than individuals alone

Smith MJ et al. (2014). The scientific impact of nations: Journal placement and citation performance. *PLoS One.* 9(10): e109195.
- Internationally-diverse scientific teams produce better research

PART ONE: CRAFT A COMPELLING VISION

Bass BM, Steidlmeier P. (1999). Ethics, character, and authentic transformational leadership behavior. *Leadership Quarterly.* 10(2): 181–217.
- Transformational leadership depends on the moral character of leaders, the ethical values in their visions, and the morality of their methods

Carton AM, Murphy C, Clark JR. (2014). A (blurry) vision of the future: how leader rhetoric about ultimate goals influences performance. *Acad Manag J.* 57(6): 1544–1570.
- A vision of the future establishes a shared sense of purpose and boosts performance
- The best messages include a large amount of vision imagery combined with a small number of values

Stam D, van Knippenberg D, Wisse B. (2010). Focusing on followers: the role of regulatory focus and possible selves in visionary leadership. *Leadersh Q.* 21(3): 457–468.
- A vision invites followers to create an ideal self and work towards making it a reality

Griffin MA, Parker SK, Mason CM. (2010). Leader vision and the development of adaptive and proactive performance: a longitudinal study. *J Appl Psychol.* 95(1): 174–182.
- Emphasizing a vision leads to more adaptability and openness within the organization

Hulsheger UR, Anderson N, Salgado JF. (2009). Team-level predictors of innovation at work: a comprehensive meta-analysis spanning three decades of research. *J Appl Psychol.* 94(5): 1128–1145.
- Vision predicts greater team creativity and innovation

Arnoux-Nicolas C et al. (2015). Perceived work conditions and turnover intentions: The mediating role of meaning of work. *Front Psychol.* 7: 704.
- Meaning of work connects people to a cause larger than themselves and lowers turnover intentions

Kahneman D et al. (2003). A perspective on judgment and choice: mapping bounded rationality. *Am Psychol.* 58(9): 697–720.
- Your brain uses two systems for thinking:
  - System 1: fast, intuitive, and emotional
  - System 2: slow, calculating, and logical

Luo J, Yu Rongjun. (2015). Follow the heart or the head? The interactive influence model of emotion and cognition. *Front Psychol.* 6: 573.
- Emotion is often stronger than logic, especially when there is incomplete information, limited decision time, and ego depletion
- Emotional response is strengthened by immediate threats or rewards, self-related information, and social stimuli

Baumeister RF et al. (2001). Bad is stronger than good. *Review of General Psychology.* 5(4): 323-370.
- Negative emotions are stronger than positive ones

Tannenbaum MB et al. (2015). Appealing to fear: A meta-analysis of fear appeal effectiveness and theories. *Psychol Bull.* 141(6): 1178-1204.
- Appealing to fear is highly effective at influencing attitudes, intentions, and behaviors
- The effect is increased if the appeal is coupled with solutions

Job RFS. (1988). Effective and ineffective use of fear in health promotion campaigns. *Am J Public Health.* 78(2): 163-167.
- For health promotion campaigns, appealing to fear is effective if it is combined with a specific recommended behavior to reduce the fear

Morris JD et al. (2002). The power of affect: Predicting intention. *Journal of Advertising Research.* 42(3): 7-17.
- In a study of 23,000 responses to 240 advertising messages, emotional response predicted intentions and actions much better than logical response

Coleman NV, Williams P. (2015). Looking for my self: Identity-driven attention allocation. *Journal of Consumer Psychology.* 25(3): 504-511.
- People focus their attention on cues and stimuli that are consistent with their social identities

Burnkrant RE, Unnava HR. (1989). Self-referencing: A strategy for increasing processing of message content. *Personality and Social Psychology Bulletin.* 15(4): 628-638.
- Self-referencing messages are more persuasive

Vastfjall D et al. (2014). Compassion fade: Affect and charity are greatest for a single child in need. *PLoS One.* 9(6): e100115.
- People's capacity to feel sympathy for others in need is limited and compassion fatigue leads to apathy and inaction
- Sympathy and charity is highest for a single child in need

Cameron CD, Payne BK. (2011). Escaping affect: how motivated emotion regulation creates insensitivity to mass suffering. *J Pers Soc Psychol.* 100(1): 1-15.
- People are insensitive to mass suffering to avoid being overwhelmed by emotions

Sopory P, Dillard JP. (2002). The persuasive effects of metaphor: A meta-analysis. *Human Communication Research.* 28(3): 382–419.
- Metaphor helps structure and organize the arguments of a message
- It is more persuasive to use a single familiar metaphor than multiple ones

Thibodeau PH, Boroditsky L. (2011). Metaphors we think with: the role of metaphor in reasoning. *PLoS One.* 6(2): e16782.
- Metaphors create a frame and encourage people to make inferences consistent with the frame

Bai M. (2005, July 17). The framing wars. *New York Times.*
- "tax relief" is a frame that suggests we are being oppressed by taxes and need to be liberated from them

Oppenheimer DM. (2005). Consequences of erudite vernacular utilized irrespective of necessity: problems with using long words needlessly. *Applied Cognitive Psychology.* 20(2): 139–156.
- Authors who use complex words are judged to be less intelligent

Reber R, Schwarz N. (1999). Effects of perceptual fluency on judgments of truth. *Conscious Cogn.* 8(3): 338–342.
- Easy-to-read statements are perceived as being more truthful

McGlone MS, Tofighbakhsh J. (2000). Birds of a feather flock conjointly (?): rhyme as reason in aphorisms. *Psychol Sci.* 11(5): 424–428.
- Rhymes increases perception of truthfulness

Obermeier C et al. (2013). Aesthetic and emotional effects of meter and rhyme in poetry. *Front Psychol.* 4: 10.
- Rhymes lead to more positive emotions

Lea RB et al. (2008). Sweet silent thought: alliteration and resonance in poetry comprehension. *Psychol Sci.* 19(7): 709–716.
- Alliteration is memorable

Warning: With great persuasive power comes great responsibility

Cialdini RB, Petrova PK, Goldstein NJ. (2004). The hidden costs of organizational dishonesty. *MIT Sloan Management Review.* 45(3): 67–73.
- Dishonest companies may generate short-term profits, but they incur long-term costs:
    o Poor reputation leads to less return business and lower long-term profits
    o Mismatch with employee values leads to higher stress and absenteeism, low job satisfaction, and high turnover
    o The remaining dishonest employees require increased surveillance to prevent stealing and kickbacks

Ambrose ML, Arnaud A, Schminke M. (2008). Individual moral development and ethical climate: The influence of person–organization fit on job attitudes. *Journal of Business Ethics*. 77(3): 323–333.
- Employees in unethical companies have lower job satisfaction and higher turnover intentions

Pinto J, Leana CR, Pil FK. (2008). Corrupt organizations or organizations of corrupt individuals? Two types of organization-level corruption. Acad Manage Rev. 33(3): 685–709.
- Corruption is contagious in an organization

Darke PR, Ritchie RJB. (2007). The defensive consumer: Advertising deception, defensive processing, and distrust. *Journal of Marketing Research*. 44(1): 114–127.
- Deceptive advertising undermines the credibility of future advertising

Nguyen N, Leblanc G. (2001). Corporate image and corporate reputation in customers' retention decisions in services. *Journal of Retailing and Consumer Services*. 8(4): 227–236.
- Customers are more loyal to companies with good corporate reputations and corporate images

Trudel R, Cotte . (2009). Does it pay to be good? *MIT Sloan Management Review*. 50(2): 61–68.
- Customers pay less money for products from unethical companies

PART TWO: RECRUIT THE BEST TEAM

Intelligence

Gottfredson LS et al. (2002). Where and why g matters: Not a mystery. *Human Performance*. 15(1): 25–46.
- Intelligence is the general capability for processing complex information and predicts performance better for high-complexity jobs

Gottfredson LS et al. (1997). Why g matters: The complexity of everyday life. *Intelligence*. 24(1): 79–132.
- Intelligence is the ability to deal with cognitive complexity
- The more complex a work task, the greater the advantages of high intelligence

Robertson KF et al. (2010). Beyond the threshold hypothesis: Even among the gifted and top math/science graduate students, cognitive abilities, vocational interests, and lifestyle preferences matter for career choice, performance, and persistence. *Current Directions in Psychological Science*. 19(6): 346–351.
- The higher one's cognitive ability, the higher the likelihood of achievement in education, career, and creative outcomes

Schmidt FL, Hunter J. (2004). General mental ability in the world of work: occupational attainment and job performance. *J Pers Soc Psychol.* 86(1): 162–173.
- Intelligence is more important than conscientiousness at predicting job performance

Kuncel NR, Hezlett SA. (2010). Fact and fiction in cognitive ability testing for admissions and hiring decisions. *Current Directions in Psychological Science.* 19(6): 339–345.
- Intelligence predicts higher creativity and leadership

Alexander J, Smales S. (1997). Intelligence, learning and long-term memory. *Personality and Individual Differences.* 23(5): 815–825.
- Intelligent people learn faster

Lee H et al. (2015). The relationship between intelligence and training gains is moderated by training strategy. *PLoS One.* 10(4): e0123259.
- Intelligent people mastered a complex game faster

Barrick MR et al. (1998). Relating member ability and personality to work-team processes and team effectiveness. *J Appl Psychol.* 83(3): 377–391.
- Teams that had higher intelligence and conscientiousness received higher supervisor ratings for performance

Devine DJ, Philips JL. (2001). Do smarter teams do better: A meta-analysis of cognitive ability and team performance. *Small Group Research.* 32(5): 507–532.
- Smarter teams perform better

Judge TA et al. (2007). Self-efficacy and work-related performance: the integral role of individual differences. *J Appl Psychol.* 92(1): 107–127.
- Self-efficacy has minimal predictive power for job performance above and beyond intelligence and conscientiousness

Wonderlic test. (n.d.). In *Wikipedia.* Retrieved July 23, 2020, from https://en.wikipedia.org/wiki/Wonderlic_test
- Lists average scores for the 12-minute 50-question test

Conscientiousness and grit

Heckman JJ, Kautz T. (2012). Hard evidence on soft skills. *Labour Econ.* 19(4): 451–464.
- Conscientiousness is defined as "the tendency to be organized, responsible, and hardworking" and is related to grit, perseverance, delay of gratification, impulse control, achievement striving, ambition, and work ethic
- Conscientiousness increases with age

Dudley NM et al. (2006). A meta-analytic investigation of conscientiousness in the prediction of job performance: examining the intercorrelations and the incremental validity of narrow traits. *J Appl Psychol.* 91(1): 40–57.
- Conscientiousness predicts job performance

Neuman GA, Wright J. (1999). Team effectiveness: beyond skills and cognitive ability. *J Appl Psychol.* 84(3): 376–389.
- Agreeableness and conscientiousness predict supervisor ratings of team performance

Judge TA et al. (2002). Personality and leadership: a qualitative and quantitative review. *J Appl Psychol.* 87(4): 765–780.
- Leadership is associated with conscientiousness

Crede M, Tynan MC, Harms PD. (2016). Much ado about grit: A meta-analytic synthesis of the grit literature. *J Pers Soc Psychol.* 113(3): 492–511.
- Grit is a subcomponent of conscientiousness
- The most important aspect of grit is perseverance

Jackson JJ et al. (2010). What do conscientious people do? Development and validation of the Behavioral Indicators of Conscientiousness (BIC). *J Res Pers.* 44(4): 501–511.
- Conscientious people are more likely to do the following behaviors: label drawers in my office, use a planner to schedule the days' events, cross off items from my to do list, make an itinerary, file papers in a desk drawer, make lists, use a calendar or date book to plan my activities, file financial documents, organize work files and materials in a systematic manner, use a file system for important papers, write in a date book, set a timeline for getting a project done, persist at tasks after meeting setbacks or failures, work extra hard on a project to make sure that it is done right, complete the projects I start, get to appointments on time, allow extra time for getting lost when going to new places, complete assignments on time, show up for work more than 5 min early, get to work on time, return phone calls and emails in a timely fashion, keep up with required work, fulfill an obligation to someone, double-check my work, proofread my writing, pay bills on time

Integrity

Schmidt FL, Hunter JE. (1998). The validity and utility of selection methods in personnel psychology: Practical and theoretical implications of 85 years of research findings. *Psychological Bulletin.* 124(2): 262–274.
- Intelligence, conscientiousness, and integrity are strong predictors of job performance

DeTienne KB et al. (2012). The impact of moral stress compared to other stressors on employee fatigue, job satisfaction, and turnover: An empirical investigation. *Journal of Business Ethics.* 110(3): 377–391.
- Moral stress increased employee fatigue and turnover intention and decreased job satisfaction

Mayer DM et al. (2009). How low does ethical leadership flow? Test of a trickle-down model. *Organizational Behavior and Human Decision Processes.* 108: 1–13.
- Ethical leadership flows from management to employees

Dirks KT, Ferrin DL. (2002). Trust in leadership: Meta-analytic findings and implications for research and practice. *Journal of Applied Psychology.* 87(4): 611–628.
- Trust in one's direct manager predicts job satisfaction, organizational commitment, and reduces turnover intention

Kaiser RB, Hogan R. (2010). How to (and how not to) assess the integrity of managers. *Consulting Psychology Journal: Practice and Research.* 62(4): 216–234.
- An effective way to assess integrity is to ask employees the likelihood that their manager would behave unethically if given the opportunity

Emotional intelligence

Mayer JD, Salovey P. (1993). The intelligence of emotional intelligence. *Intelligence.* 17(4): 433–442.
- Emotional intelligence involves the ability to monitor one's own and others' emotions, to discriminate among them, and to use the information to guide one's thinking and actions

Ghosh R, Shuck B, Petrosko J. (2012). Emotional intelligence and organizational learning in work teams. *Journal of Management Development.* 31(6): 603–619.
- High levels of emotional intelligence enable team members to be aware and reflective of each other's emotions and to manage each other's emotions
- This allows people to express themselves in a psychologically safe environment, resulting in better team learning and higher productivity

Edmondson AC, Lei Z. (2014). Psychological safety: The history, renaissance, and future of an interpersonal construct. *Annu Rev Organ Psychol Organ Behav.* 1: 23–43.
- Teams with higher psychological safety perform better, learn faster, have lower turnover, and individuals are more likely to speak up
- People are more likely to offer ideas, admit mistakes, ask for help, or provide feedback if they believe it is safe to do so

Edmondson A. (1999). Psychological safety and learning behavior in work teams. *Administrative Science Quarterly.* 44(2): 350–383.
- Psychological safety describes a climate of interpersonal trust and mutual respect in which people are comfortable being themselves
- Teams learned faster when they had higher psychological safety

Woolley AW et al. (2010). Evidence for a collective intelligence factor in the performance of human groups. *Science.* 330(6004): 686–688.
- Group performance is predicted by average social sensitivity of group members, equality in taking turns during conversations, and proportion of women in the group

Engel D et al. (2017). What makes a strong team? Using collective intelligence to predict team performance in League of Legends. *CSCW '17 Proceedings of the 2017 ACM Conference on Computer Supported Cooperative Work and Social Computing.* Pages 2316–2329.
- Higher social perceptiveness and collective intelligence are associated with higher team performance in League of Legends, the most popular video game in the world

Brunetto Y et al. (2012). Emotional intelligence, job satisfaction, well-being and engagement: explaining organizational commitment and turnover intentions in policing. *Human Resource Management Journal.* 22(4): 428–441.
- In a study of police officers, emotional intelligence led to job satisfaction and well-being and lowered turnover intentions

Baron-Cohen S et al. (2001). The "Reading the Mind in the Eyes" Test revised version: a study with normal adults, and adults with Asperger syndrome or high-functioning autism. *J Child Psychol Psychiatry.* 42(2): 241–251.
- The Reading the Mind in the Eyes test consists of 36 photos with 4 answer choices for each photo
- The average score is 26.4 for women and 26.0 for men
- The average score is 21.9 for people with Asperger syndrome or high-functioning autism

Engel D et al. (2014). Reading the Mind in the Eyes or reading between the lines? Theory of Mind predicts collective intelligence equally well online and face-to-face. *PLoS One.* 9(12): e115212.
- The Reading the Mind in the Eyes test is a reliable way to assess emotional intelligence

Olderbak S et al. (2015). A psychometric analysis of the reading the mind in the eyes test: toward a brief form for research and applied settings. *Front Psychol.* 6: 1503.
- The Reading the Mind in the Eyes test is related to Cognitive Empathy and Emotion Perception

Riess H et al. (2012). Empathy training for resident physicians: a randomized controlled trial of a neuroscience-informed curriculum. *J Gen Intern Med.* 27(10): 1280–1286.
- The skill of decoding subtle facial expressions can be significantly improved with training

PART THREE: BE A GREAT MANAGER

Judge TA, Piccolo RF, Ilies R. (2004). The forgotten ones? The validity of consideration and initiating structure in leadership research. *J Appl Psychol.* 89(1): 36–51.
- Leader performance is predicted by Consideration (showing concern and respect, looking out for others' welfare, and expressing appreciation and support) and Initiating Structure (defining and organizing roles, setting goals,

establishing patterns and channels of communication)

Gerstner CR, Day DV. (1997). Meta-analytic review of leader-member exchange theory: Correlates and construct issues. *J Appl Psychol.* 82(6): 827–844.
- The quality of the relationship between a leader and a team member predicts job performance, job satisfaction, commitment, and turnover intentions

Bryant A. (2011, March 12). Google's quest to build a better boss. *New York Times.*

Morgeson FP, DeRue DS, Karam EP. (2010). Leadership in teams: A functional approach to understanding leadership structures and processes. *Journal of Management.* 36(1): 5–39.
- Leadership functions include choosing team members, defining the mission, establishing expectations and goals, creating a structure and plan, training and developing the team, managing how the team thinks about important events, providing feedback, monitoring the team, managing team boundaries, challenging the team, solving problems, providing resources, and supporting the social climate

Kozlowski SWJ, Ilgen DR. (2006). Enhancing the effectiveness of work groups and teams. *Psychological Science in the Public Interest.* 7(3): 77–124.
- Leaders can increase team performance through task-focused and team-development focused behaviors
- Leaders can motivate team members by using recognition and rewards for achieving goals

Bryant A. (2013, August 1). Luc Levesque of Trip Advisor, on frequent evaluations. *New York Times.*
- Perform 30-day assessments with your team members

www.ingramcontent.com/pod-product-compliance
Lightning Source LLC
Chambersburg PA
CBHW071405210526
45465CB00001B/260